Christmas Party Celebrations

71
New and
Exciting
Party Plans
for
Holiday Fun

Denise Distel Dytrych

Brighton Publications

Brighton Publications, Inc.

Brighton Publications, Inc.
P.O. Box 120706
St. Paul, MN 55112-0706
612-636-2220

First Edition: 1997

Library of Congress Cataloging-in-Publication Data
Dytrych, Denise Distell
    [1st ed]
    Christmas party celebrations : 71 new and exciting party
plans for holiday fun / Denise Distel Dytrych.
        p.   cm.
    Includes bibliographical references and index.
    1. Christmas—United States. 2. Holidays—United
States—Planning. 3. Entertaining—United States—Planning.
4. United States—Social life and customs. I. Title.
GT4986.A1D97   1997   97-22238
792.2'2—dc21   CIP

ISBN 0-918420-33-4

Printed in the United States of America

This book is dedicated to my husband
Terry
with whom every day is a celebration.

Preface

Sometimes it's difficult to break away from what we've been so well trained to do. Our minds are always racing ahead, yet we never cross the finish line because there's always another race we join, usually while we're catching our breath from the last one. It's not uncommon to juggle many different projects at the same time. And we're so darn good at it. But, at what cost?

Between work and family commitments, it's hard to find time to do anything just for the pure pleasure of it. One thing is certain. You will never "find" time nor will you "make" time. What we have is all there is. What we can do, however, is decide what's important and prioritize our commitments. We have to learn to go for quality, not quantity. Life is way too short. I know you've heard that before. But do you believe it? You can't afford not to. You can't afford to do things because "you should," because "you have to because that's the way it is," and, the worst excuse of all, because "what will others think if I do?" Who cares! It's your life.

Decide today that you're going to take life a little less seriously. I'm not suggesting you become lax on important matters. I'm suggesting that you spend some of your time having fun. Doing something just because you want to, regardless of what others may think. In other words, don't merely exist. Start living your life the way you want to. It really is way too short and it's very precious.

I hope you enjoy this book as much as I enjoyed writing it. Most importantly, enjoy your life. Celebrate every thing every day!

Denise Distel Dytrych
Palm Beach, Florida
June, 1997

Contents

Introduction

Do you believe in Santa Claus? If you do — hooray! This book is definitely for you. If you gave up on Santa Claus when you discovered that the tooth fairy was really your mother — how about magic? Do you believe in it? You know — abracadabra, hocus pocus? No? Well, do you believe in . . . having a great time? I thought so! Now we're all on the same sheet of music (and I'm not talking "Silent Night" — I'm talking "Jingle Bells" in a big way, all the way)! I believe in it all — Santa Claus, magic, the tooth fairy — especially having a great time. That's why I decided to write this book.

I was at the point of exhaustion with the same old get-togethers. Every dinner party, every cocktail reception, every black-tie affair seemed to merge one into the other into the other, until they all became one! This is especially true during the holidays. It's not unusual to attend at least four functions a week during the season. I found myself asking, "When will this end? How long have we been here? Can we go now? Haven't we been here before — like just yesterday?" Déjà vu and vu and vu . . . whew! Where is the new and exciting?

It's here. And it's here for you. For you who believe in Santa Claus, for you who believe in the magic of the season, and for you who want to spread good cheer to family and friends — touching them with the joy and excitement the holidays inspire. It's here even for those who think the hocus pocus stuff a bit too much. In that case, it's for you who believe in a reason, any reason, to party and who are willing to shed the conventional way of doing things.

Forget what you've been programmed to think and do in the name of what is "proper" and "acceptable." According to whom? You know what I'm talking about. Having to be every thing to every body every day in every way. No wonder we're a frazzled, uptight society. We put such a destructive strain on ourselves when we live the way we should because others tell us we must. Who are these other people? And how do they know what you or I should do? What's wrong with being yourself? Following your gut, brain, and heart. You do not have to agree to be pulled in a hundred directions like a piece of saltwater taffy, no matter what the flavor of the day may be. Forget it! From this moment forward, revel in knowing that you do not have to do anything that no longer works for you.

Keep an open mind as you flip through the pages of this book. Give yourself this gift during the holidays to use throughout the year and the rest of your life. Promise yourself that you'll take things in stride and not sweat the small stuff. Vow that you'll start to have fun. Laugh. Play. Throw wild and crazy parties. And throw them now!

December is a big month for celebrations of all kinds. That's why it's usually so hectic. However it's not hectic because of all the things that are going on. It only becomes hectic as you make decisions on how you will deal with all those things. You're in control. Forget all the things you "should" do. You either have to really do something or you do something because you want to. Why not start looking at December in a different light? What better month to kick back, lighten up, drop your guard. Revert to childhood. I don't mean that you all of a sudden abandon all your cares in the world, quit your job, and hang out on a bench all day. I mean you might try looking at the world through a child's eyes. See the beauty in the simplest of things. Treasure things you can't see or touch. Feel the excitement a child feels waiting for Santa and his reindeer to visit. Believe that reindeers can fly and this amazing being who watches over all of us really exists.

What activities of the season excite you? The aroma of freshly baked chocolate chip cookies? The joy you experience when watching those little chocolate-studded balls through the glass in the oven door flatten into non-alien saucers oozing chocolate from select spots? Decorating the tree, adorning it with garlands you made yourself by "sewing" popcorn and cranberries together with a needle and thread? Draping the tree with the paper chains you made in art class, using strips of green and red construction paper, or sometimes using a rainbow of colors just because you thought it would be fun and different to do so? Playing with a toy train as it chugs around the base of the tree? Sneaking a peek at your gifts? Sipping hot chocolate — a jumbo marshmallow bobbing like a little white pillow that quickly disappears into the hot liquid when swirled with a candy cane? Snuggling under an old warm quilt in front of a roaring fire reading *Twas The Night Before Christmas?* Seeing *The Nutcracker* ballet — imagining that you are one of the sugar plum fairies leaping across the fantasy strewn stage? Watching your favorite Christmas movies and programs? There are millions of these scenarios. They are yours for the imagining.

Think about what you always did or always wanted to do as a child, and do it. The party ideas you'll find in the pages to follow are designed to capture the spirit of youth that resides in each one of us whether you like it or not. Let that child come out to play this holiday season. (But, since we're grown-ups nonetheless, some of the innocence of youth has been intentionally omitted from the party plans!) The point is to have fun . . . create your own memories whether they're from what you already know and love or from what you always wished upon a star for — the time is now!

Some ideas may seem far-fetched, too childish, and perhaps downright ridiculous, if not absurd — "we are adults after all," some may sniff! But wait . . . we all like to have fun. We have to have fun. It's a requirement of life if we're really living. Good times are great releases from everyday pressures. Do you remember when you couldn't wait to be an adult so that you could do whatever you wanted to do? Stay up all night — eat sweets until your belly ached — run with scissors? Well, it happened. Here you are. (*Note:* It's probably still a good idea to not run with scissors.) Aren't we quite the serious folk in our day-to-day lives? Enough of that stuffy stuff I say! Let there be no limits. Throw out the rules. Within these pages, you'll find invitations, decorations, menu ideas, and more for 71 holiday parties. That's more than enough to throw at least two parties a day during the month of December right through January 1st. The rest is up to you. Skim through the plans and find what interests you. Introduce the ideas to your imagination and see what happens. Don't be shy. It's impossible to do anything wrong (unless you forget the invitation step).

These parties are a mix of humor, fantasy, and plain old fun, seasoned with the spirit of Christmas. They were created to help us keep what surrounds and consumes us in perspective. If you haven't already noticed, I believe that life is too short to do the accepted normal thing, whatever "normal" is. Reject the same old, same old. Long gone are the uptight days of Swedish meatballs swimming in a crock pot and stale saltines with cubes of oily cheese lying listlessly on a platter. Say "hello" to what hasn't been done yet, and welcome the excitement of doing the unusual with open arms. Everything that surrounds you is special, even the simple things. It's a matter of how you look at them. Re-name the ordinary and it automatically becomes something special and worth celebrating. I urge you not to merely exist in this world of ours. It's a wonderful place. Start living your life purely for the fun of it.

When you get right down to it, most parties are a piece of cake. I don't mean that they're a breeze to pull together. It just seems to me that there's something missing. Here's what I've concluded. Surely you've heard something referred to as "the icing on the cake." That something is usually a very good thing. For example, you get your paycheck as you always do. That's a good thing because you have bills to pay. You're content. And then one day something is different. You go to deposit your check and discover there's an extra hundred bucks in your paycheck. Wow! Isn't that nice! A pleasant surprise. Something you weren't expecting. A very good thing. Well, that 100 dollar bonus is the icing.

The secret to a successful, never-to-be-forgotten party, is a well-iced cake. That's what will separate your party from all the other parties. In spite of this revelation, the cake is very important and will be discussed in the following section aptly titled "The Cake." So, when you see "The Cake" referenced in the plans, turn to this section for general, starting point tips. "The Icing" can be found in Chapters 2 through 17. Each chapter contains party ideas I've grouped in broad categories, ranging from traditional to sports to international to noisemakers. You'll find all sorts of ideas that are sure to tickle your fancy. A list of resources and references for books, companies, and magazines are at the end. I suggest you check it out for additional ideas.

So, grab some paper and something to write with — it's party time!

Chapter 1

The Cake

By the time you breeze through this chapter you'll know everything you need to know to throw a party. This is where you'll learn the basics. In other words, you'll know how to bake the Cake.

The recipe for a basic party consists of eleven general ingredients. I'll tell you what the ingredients are; however, the actual preparation of the cake is up to you. Armed with all the ingredients, you decide how you want to prepare them — blend, toss, puree, fry, broil, shake 'n' bake, or serve 'em raw. There is no one right way to do things when it comes to partying. Your way is the only way when it's something you're putting together. Let's go through each of the ingredients. It's helpful to start a separate sheet of paper for each one of the steps. Jot down any ideas when they pop into your head. Don't judge what you're thinking. Just record the idea and move on. It's time to create some magic.

Theme

Select a theme. Go through the party ideas in Chapters 2 through 17 and find one that grabs you. You now have a theme, and don't you forget it!

Guest List

Make a guest list. As you put pen to paper, don't lose sight of your theme. I believe that everyone can have a great time; however, even the best of friends can be party poopers if they aren't in to what you're up to. So, in the name of good times had by all, don't feel bad about politely drawing a line through the name of any person that might not share your sense of humor or zest for a particular party you'd like to throw. The worst thing that can happen is that person will politely cross you off their list.

Location

Select a location. The number of guests and, once again, that theme, will drive this decision. Your home, community clubhouse, restaurant, hotel meeting room or ballroom, office, park, ice rink, beach, bowling alley — you name it — there's a perfect place for your party. Throughout the party ideas I refer to the "party area." This covers the entire area your guests will have access to, including medicine chests.

Budget

Establish a budget. A gathering of friends should be relaxing and fun. It shouldn't bankrupt you. There's no point in adding stress when working on something that's supposed to help you alleviate it, so decide how much you want to spend and don't waver. You can always revise the party plans to fit your budget. There's a less expensive alternative to everything I've suggested. Consider sharing the costs by co-hosting the bash with a friend or two.

Time

Determine the best time to hold your party. Keep your theme in mind (how could you forget)? Breakfast, lunch, brunch, dinner, happy hour, or all of the above. Each event can be centered on any of these traditional gathering times — or create your own! How about dessert at the stroke of midnight? Or an eye-opener at dawn where assorted coffees and cakes are served?

Invitations

Now it's time to think about your invitations. Each invitation should include: • the name(s) of the person(s) hosting the party • the theme • the day, date, and time • the place • directions • R.S.V.P. telephone number and the name of your social secretary (usually the same as yours). If your guests' attire is part of your plan, designate the suggested dress code on the invitation. Attire is usually designated as "formal," "black tie," "black tie optional," "cocktail," or "casual." You will be introduced to a whole new line of designations, as you'll see soon enough when you are ready for the Icing. (The interpretations are surely to be amusing.) Don't forget to include any special instructions, for example: "Bring an unwrapped gift," "Don't forget to bring a batch of cookies," or "Wear Only A Sombrero."

Some envelopes will require extra postage. It's a good idea to take your invitations to the post office to be weighed to make sure you are covered. (I don't know what would be worse — the invitations never being delivered or returned to you the day after your party, or the recipient being asked to pay the postage due! Let's not be in the position of having to pick one.) If you decide to use paper invitations, you are no longer limited to those standard fill-in-the-blank cards. With the introduction of computer generated cards, you can customize your selection. You can print anything, and I mean anything, on your invitation. You select the card you'd like to send, input your message into the computer, and wait a few moments to receive cards made just for you. These incredible machines can be found at many locations, including card shops and chain drugstores.

I've suggested quite a few invitation ideas that border on the extravagant as I believe the invitation sets the tone for what's to come. Many of the invitation ideas will have to be hand-delivered or mailed in a box or a tube. To easily draw attention to your invitations, add some confetti or other surprises before sealing the envelope flap, capping the mailing tube, or taping the box shut. Confetti is made from paper, plastic, or sequin-like material. It comes in a variety of shapes and colors. Party outlet stores seem to have the best selection. The shower of sparkly stuff as the package is opened leaves quite an impression (the nature and extent of which depends on what your potential guest is wearing and where that person is located when your invitation is opened)! In any event, your guests will get the message that your party is not to be missed!

I use the words "printed invitation" throughout the plans. When you see this, I'm referring to any regular paper invitations that you make, buy off the rack, or computer generate. Oftentimes I'll suggest that you "attach" something to a printed invitation. You can do this with staples, glue, tape, even a ribbon threaded through a hole you make — whatever works with the materials you are using.

Plan on sending the invitations out at least four weeks prior to the big day. This is especially important during the holiday season. There's a lot going on and you want to make sure that everyone comes to your party.

Decorations

The next step is to plan your decorations, both indoors and outdoors. Go for everything and anything that will stimulate your guests' senses, spark their imagination, and carry forward your chosen theme with flying colors (and whatever else you want flying around — there are no limits to what you can do). Here is a list of some basic decorations to get the ball rolling:

Wreaths — real or artificial, evergreen or grapevine — to hang on doors and in windows

Garlands — ropes of greenery and tinsel to wrap around banisters, columns, lampposts, swing sets, and to frame windows, doorways, and serving tables

Ribbons and bows — French-wired, gold and silver cording, grosgrain, lace, moiré, plaid, taffeta, satin, jute string, and organza — to tie around and on candlesticks, chandeliers, sconces, and lamp bases; basket and pitcher handles; chair backs; houseplants and tree limbs — basically anything that sticks up and out

Balloons, streamers, and banners — solids, patterns, mylar, imprinted with a message, in all colors or Christmas red and green — to tie on to objects or to float anywhere in the party area

Centerpieces — consider floral arrangements in red, green, and white carnations (they seem to last forever), roses, lilies, amaryllis; twigs, pussy willows, and eucalyptus branches; ferns in decorated containers; and ice sculptures. Decorate tabletop size Christmas trees with items that carry out your theme (bells, cookies, Santas).

Lighting — luminaries placed along your driveway, walkway, patio, porch, or any other outdoor area. All you need are lunch-size paper bags with shapes of stars or other forms cut out from one side of the bag to allow the candle to shine through — you can make these yourself or buy through a catalog or from a party supply outlet. Fill the bags a third of the way with sand and place a votive or tea candle inside the bag. You can also use small clay flowerpots. Here are some other lighting ideas: String miniature white lights everywhere. Replace standard light bulbs with red and/or green bulbs. Drape lamp shades with squares of tulle, gauze, or organza to create a soft, muted glow.

Candles, candles, candles. Even though candles are considered to be sources of light, I believe they are so much more. They instantly create a relaxing atmosphere and are appropriate for any kind of party. Buy taper, pillar, cake, tea, and votive candles by the box. Safely place throughout the party area.

Don't forget **scents**. Bowls and baskets of potpourri. Simmer orange sections, cloves, and cinnamon sticks in a large pot of water on your stove. Candles scented with pine, cranberry, cinnamon, and spice are some popular holiday aromas.

There are a couple of items you won't want to be without that can single-handedly transform the every day into holiday glitz. Pick up some gold and silver spray paint to bring the holidays to pine cones, tree limbs, pine boughs, and baskets. The other item is a hot glue gun. You'll be able to attach almost anything to everything with it. If you make a mistake, the object can be peeled right off. This glue is very forgiving.

The decoration ideas you just read apply to both the inside and the outside of the party area. The specific party ideas are geared more towards the indoors, so I thought I'd make some general outdoor suggestions. You want to make your party location enticing. You want to seduce your guests with a tease of garland and some twinkling lights. Like the bat of an eye, or an alluring glance, your guests will be drawn into the party where the theme decorations will really knock their socks off. You want your guests to do a double-take the moment they arrive in the area. Try to get a little "ah-oh-ah-wow" reaction. Some oohs and ahs like Meg Ryan belted out in the movie, *When Harry Met Sally.* You really don't have to do much. I've discovered that lights alone make a huge impact. The only suggestion I have if you decide to put up lights, is to make sure you use only one kind. Go all white, all colors, all twinkling. It gets a bit too busy and takes away from what you are trying to accomplish when different kinds of strands are used. To finish the outside decorations, put a wreath on the entrance door. Wrap some greenery with ribbons around the mailbox, lantern, lamppost, and handrails. Trim the window frames with lights and garland. Spray on some artificial snow. Add a touch of your theme.

Plates, cups, napkins, tablecloths, utensils, and serving pieces are considered decorations. All should be visually appealing and play a large part in carrying out your theme. They are available in solids and patterns, in a rainbow of colors or simply clear. Choose from paper, plastic, metal, fabric, wood, or glass — a variety of finishes. Check out fabric stores for holiday material. Bolts of festive fabrics find their way to the sales floor in time for holiday celebrations. Use for tablecloths and runners (a piece of cloth about a third of the width of your table that can be placed lengthwise or across, or both runners are an effective way to incorporate prints that otherwise may be too overwhelming). Fabrics in solid red and green, and silver and gold lamé can be topped with lace or crocheted tablecloths in ivory or white, gold or silver. For the finishing touch, sprinkle confetti, feathers, glitter, and other sparklies across the top of the serving table. Imprint cocktail napkins, matches, and tumblers with some of the party information. Roll utensils in a napkin, tie with raffia or ribbon, and insert a candy cane, a cinnamon stick, or a sprig of holly in the knot. Display the bundles in a clever container.

Baskets are my favorite serving containers. They are inexpensive and come in a variety of shapes, sizes, and colors. Baskets can be used over and over again. Hang them on a wall or display them on shelves and counter tops, or on the top of cabinets or a kitchen hutch when you're not partying. When you are, simply line whatever basket you want to use with a cloth or paper napkin, or some straw or shredded tissue paper depending on your theme (that theme again!) and the food to be served. Tie ribbons and bows to the handles, letting them flow down and around the tabletop, encircling the items on the table. Weave battery-operated miniature lights (available at craft stores) into or around the baskets — a magical display when the area lights are dimmed.

There will come a point during your party when your guests will want to sit down, no matter how much fun they are having mingling and dancing the morning away. Mix and match tables and chairs you already have. Here's another solution. You've heard of B.Y.O.B.? Well, we're moving up the alphabet to the world of B.Y.O.C. (Bring Your Own Chair). If this is out of the question, borrow some chairs from friends and neighbors, or rent some from a party supplier. Don't forget that the floor is also a seating option. Toss some throw pillows — once again, what's your theme?

The borrow or rent suggestion goes for everything you need for your party. You can always rent what you don't have and what you haven't been able to beg, borrow, or steal (of course, you never would).

Even though I've emphasized the importance of keeping your chosen theme in mind while planning your party, don't go overboard. As with everything else in life, too much of a good thing is not a good thing! You'll know when you've reached that distracting point. Incorporate decor that will carry out your plan with the traditional Christmas decorations you would normally use — a Christmas tree, poinsettias, pine branches, mistletoe, baubles, garlands, and lights — all add to the festive atmosphere without smothering it. Under some plans, I state that "General Christmas" is all that's needed. When you see these words, the decorations suggested in this section are enough to create the appropriate environment.

Entertainment

Now that you have an idea of what your place will look like, think about entertainment. At the very least, provide background music. Christmas carols to cater to all types of music tastes are readily available on cassette tape and CD. Also, radio stations play continuous music that you can tune in to just by spinning the dial. Think theme! Consider handing out caroling books in case your guests feel like creating their own music by joining in a sing-a-long. Have your party group do some caroling around your neighborhood. Invite a local church or school group to stop by and sing a few tunes. If your budget can stand it, consider live music. Let your fingers do the walking through the yellow pages (you can count this as a workout during the month of December) to see what's available. A harp, piano, flute, and/or cello make beautiful music and it's a special treat to watch the musicians as they play. Hire a Santa Claus to amuse your guests. Some of the party plans suggest what "kind" of Santa would fit right in. Movies are also a great spread of holiday cheer, and it's a big treat to have an opportunity to watch one during this busy time. Plug a Christmas video into your VCR and set up a viewing area. Some people love to play games. You could play Christmas Charades ("Guess what Christmas carol character I am?") or any other group challenge. Having a contest of some sort can be very entertaining, too. I've suggested some contests in the specific plans.

Party Favors

Everyone likes a little surprise to take home with them, so include party favors in your budget. Glass jars, baskets, gift bags, and other containers full of your theme are easy-to-do favors with impact. Fill them with candy canes, peppermints, nuts, or a homemade specialty. Add a ribbon and a personalized label. Throughout the plans I'll suggest that you fill a gift bag or other container with shredded tissue. You don't have to shred the paper yourself. Bags of different colors can be found in the gift wrap section of any store. Anything personalized with your guests' names and/or the party information such as T-shirts, baseball caps, mugs, key chains, buttons, pens and pencils, gift bags, drink coolers — you name it, all make for a special memento. Be creative with your imprints. For example, order T-shirts that read: "I survived the First Annual Reindeer Glow Bowl." A company called "Personal Creations" offers over 100 personalized items. (*See* the Resource section at the end of this book for more information.)

Food & Beverage

Let's move on to what is perhaps the most important ingredient of your party — the food and beverage! Let's face it, people come to a party to eat and drink. Sure, the camaraderie is a big deal; however, without question, the munchies and liquids are a bigger deal. Usually *the* deal! This doesn't mean that the food preparation has to be difficult, time-consuming, or extravagant. Keep it simple! A buffet is the easiest way to go. Do it yourself, have it catered, or have your guests bring a dish (with something on it of course). When setting up a buffet, put the plates at the beginning of the line, with the napkins and utensils at the end (this arrangement spares your guests from juggling). Set up the beverages in a separate area. If you have lots of guests, set up food tables in different rooms so everyone doesn't gather in one spot.

As for the food, there are many tasty prepackaged and prepared items that can be served in a heartbeat. I've listed some quick and easy food and beverage ideas that you can dump or pour out of a box, bottle, jar, or bag. There are a few extra food suggestions in the specific plans. I didn't elaborate on menus or provide many recipes — all I've done is suggest a few items in the spirit of the theme. I'll leave the delicious details to the experts. There are many terrific cookbooks and magazines solely devoted to holiday cooking and baking. Check out the special holiday issues of *Woman's Day*, *Family Circle*, *Good Housekeeping*, and *Southern Living* for plenty of appealing recipes and ideas. Your menu will be driven by the time of the day or night you're holding your party. Is the time appropriate for happy hour, brunch, lunch, dinner, supper, dessert-only, cocktail (formal happy hour), picnic, or a coffee or tea bar? These are just a few of the options you have. Don't hesitate to do something different. Being different is what this book is all about.

Quick & Easy Food

The idea here is no-mess, no-stress feeding. There are plenty of quick fixes that happen to be quite tasty, too. Let's start off with some snack foods:

Mixed nuts, chips, and dips (combine a package of dry onion soup mix with some sour cream). Spread potato chips on a cookie sheet (use the thick sliced ones for the best result). Sprinkle with grated cheese of your choice and broil until bubbly. Pretzels served with assorted mustards; salsa and tortilla chips; black and green olives (without pits).

Raw vegetables including cauliflower, broccoli, carrots, snow peas, asparagus spears, zucchini and squash circles with an assortment of dips.

Fresh fruit wedged and sliced (dip the cut fruit in lemon or pineapple juice to keep them from browning) and dips.

Make Brie the star of an assorted cheese and cracker platter. Try these tasty suggestions using this wonderful cheese:

Allow one wheel of brie to soften. Arrange toasted almonds on top and drizzle with melted butter. Broil until softer and oozing. Serve with fancy crackers (right out of a fancy box).

Or, spread a wheel of this tasty cheese with a slightly moistened mix of brown sugar and chopped pecans. Broil until soft. Serve with gingersnaps (right out of the bag).

Or, wrap a wheel in thawed puff pastry, tucking the ends under. Drizzle with butter, toss on some sesame seeds, and bake at 350°F for 15 minutes. For a different taste, you can spread the cheese with raspberry jam before wrapping in pastry. Serve with slices of French bread (right off the bakery shelf).

Another versatile food is cream cheese. Buy in brick form and top with red or green pepper jelly, strawberry or raspberry jam, cocktail sauce topped with crabmeat, salsa topped with Monterey jack cheese. Serve with a cracker smorgasbord.

Popcorn is also a quick favorite. Air pop, micro pop, just pop. And do so by the bowlful. Melt a third cup of butter and add a fourth cup parmesan or grated cheddar or other cheese, or 2 tablespoons of taco seasoning. Chop apples and mix with popcorn, and toss with grated cheddar. Popcorn and dried cranberries also go well together. Think of what you love to eat and mix it with some popcorn.

Finger sandwiches are also easy to prepare. Spread some cream cheese on a slice of bread, top with black or green olive slices, and another piece of bread. Do the same thing with some deviled ham mixed with chopped apples, or some chopped eggs and caviar. The possibilities are mind-boggling. Cut the sandwiches into quarters.

Think about different ways of serving. Use pretzel sticks as skewers for your appetizers (tasty and environmentally kind). Another idea is to use Christmas cookie cutters (*See* the Resource section for information about a company that has cutters in all shapes and sizes.) to cut slices of cheese, cold cuts, and bread into festive stars, bells, candy canes, wreaths, and many other shapes of the season.

Here are some quick main dish ideas:

A soup bar with crackers, chunks of bread, croutons, salt and pepper, and other seasonings and spices.

Do it yourself shish kabobs — have skewers and bowls full of fixings (chunks of chicken, beef, lamb, shrimp, and veggies) and basting and dunking sauces.

A pancake and waffle bar with assorted syrups, butters, fruit, and other delicious toppings.

An omelet station — chop up all types of meats, cheeses, veggies, green and red peppers you name it — chop it!

A carving station featuring honey baked ham, roast turkey, and roast beef — with all the trimmings and a variety of breads and spreads.

A pasta bar with different types of pastas and sauces, garlic rolls, bread sticks, and a tossed salad.

A salad bar with all sorts of greens, veggies, toppings, dressings, crackers and bread.

A pizza bar with individual serving size pizza shells, sauce, various shredded cheeses, pepperoni slices, crumbled sausage, black olives, green peppers, mushrooms, and grated parmesan.

A sandwich board with all types of cold cuts, cheeses, bread and rolls. Lettuce leaves, onion and tomato slices, and pickle chips. Mustard, mayo, and other sandwich spreads. You can also serve egg, ham, tuna, chicken, shrimp, crab, and lobster salads.

Beverages

Make sure you offer a wide variety of beverages, both alcoholic and non-alcoholic. The rule of thumb for setting up a basic bar is to have the following on hand for every 10 guests:

half a case of wine (mix red, white, and rosé)

1 case of beer (regular and light)

3 liters of seltzer

4 liters of soft drinks (diet and regular)

2 quarts fruit juice (orange and grapefruit)

bottled mineral water (sparkling and flat)

1 bottle of champagne

If you're serving hard liquor, a fifth makes about 14 drinks. Have some lemon and lime wedges and twists and olives on hand. DON'T FORGET THE ICE! Plan on having a pound of ice per adult guest.

Here are some favorite holiday beverages:

A variety of gourmet hot chocolates topped with marshmallows served with a variety of swizzles sticks: peppermint sticks or candy canes, rock candy on a wooden stick, chocolate-coated spoons.

Apple cider, heated and served with a cinnamon stick.

Mint Zingers: Add a shot of Peppermint Schnapps® to hot chocolate, top with whipped cream and chocolate shavings (use a vegetable peeler), and plunk in a peppermint stick swizzler.

The Rummer Boy (hot buttered rum): 1 teaspoon sugar, ½ cup butter, 1 jigger of rum, 4 cloves. Fill mugs with boiling water, add buttered rum and a cinnamon stick swizzler, with a few butterscotch candies on the side.

Eggnog with and without rum or brandy, sprinkled with nutmeg and cinnamon (go ahead and buy the already prepared nog in the dairy section, no one will know the difference, especially if you pour a good brandy).

Fran's Reindeer Milk: 2 quarts eggnog, 2 quarts half & half, 1 cup amaretto, 1 cup white creme de cocoa, 1 cup Kahluá®, garnish with one pint vanilla ice cream and a sprinkle of nutmeg — serve in a tall mug. (BEWARE: This is deliciously dangerous stuff! One of those "creep-up-on-you" drinks!)

Mimosas: Champagne and fresh orange juice. Pour over crushed ice.

Deni's Champion Champagne: Pour the entire bottle (nebuchad-nezzar size — the largest bottle made — the equivalent of 20 regular bottles) of ridiculously expensive champagne into a very large crystal flute. Sip slowly but surely. (*Note 1:* If champagne isn't in your budget or it tickles your nose, you can substitute Miller Lite®). (*Note 2:* I recommend Perrier-Jouët Belle Epoque 1985 — it isn't ridiculously expensive, however it is outstanding).

Champagne with a Pucker and a Kick: 6 ounce can frozen lemonade concentrate, 750-milliliter bottle chilled champagne (3 cups); 2¾ cups unsweetened pineapple juice, chilled; 2 cups club soda, chilled; 1½ cups dry white wine, chilled; and 2 cups vanilla ice cream.
Prepare the lemonade according to the instructions on the can. Add the champagne, pineapple juice, club soda, and wine. Top with scoops of ice cream. Gently stir before serving. You'll get about 32 four ounce servings (enough for your party of four!).

A coffee bar is a great set up. You'll see it suggested throughout the specific plans. This is only one of many ways to go: Brew coffee with slivered almonds, cinnamon, or orange rind curls. Set out brandy and liqueurs to zip up the java. Java lavas include Galliano®, Kahluá, Triple Sec®, Tia Maria®, amaretto, sugar cubes, whipped cream, grated chocolate and cinnamon to spiff up the cream, cinnamon sticks, rock candy sticks, and flavored spoons (spoons dipped in chocolate or sugar — the coating melts when the spoon meets the hot liquid. You can make your own or buy at a better department store). Offer danishes and coffee cakes. Your guests will instantly perk up.

If you're thinking of serving punch in one of those large punch bowls, add an ice block or ring to jazz things up a bit. They're really simple to make. For the block, use a cardboard container that'll fit in the middle of your punch bowl, leaving plenty of space for the punch. Layer mixed fruit on the bottom, pack ice cubes on top to hold the fruit down. More fruit and more ice and on and on and on until the container is almost full. Fill with cold water and freeze. Remove from the freezer about one hour before your party to slightly thaw. Peel the cardboard away from the ice block, place in the bowl, and pour in the punch.

An ice ring is made in a mold the day before. Here's how to do it. Boil seven cups of water for one minute then let cool (this eliminates cloudiness). Pour three cups of the water into a 6-cup mold. Freeze, saving the remaining water. Arrange strawberries, sliced kiwifruit, orange, lemon, and lime slices, or herbs such as mint, or edible flowers on top of the frozen ice. Pour the remaining water on top and freeze. To unmold, let sit at room temperature for five minutes then float the cube in the punch.

As I previously mentioned, make sure you have non-alcoholic beverages on hand. Throughout the party plans, I reference different types of alcoholic drinks. I'm not advocating excessive consumption, nor do I believe one has to drink alcohol to have a good time (I've been known to have my wildest moments and thoughts after chugging an ice cold Diet Mountain Dew®!) The point is to make sure you have something for everyone. While I'm on the subject of alcoholic beverages, I know this goes without saying but it's worth repeating: Keep the number of a taxi service on hand for those guests without a designated driver. Their irresponsibility may become your responsibility if you provided the alcohol.

Desserts & Sweets

Everyone likes a sweet treat from time to time, especially during the holidays. You don't have to go berserk baking chocolate tortes or 7-layer cakes from scratch, nor do you have to whip up mousses and soufflés. There are plenty of all-time favorites that, just like your snacks and main course, come right out of the bag, box, or bakery. Consider these sweet tooth satisfiers:

Green and red M&M's® or jelly beans, candy canes, and other seasonal candies.

Cakes, cupcakes, and cookies. A cake topper bar. Buy plain cakes such as pound cake and angel food cake and serve with all sorts of delightful sauces and creams.

Cinnamon ice cream flagged with a cinnamon stick.

A sundae/cone bar — vanilla ice cream served with all sorts of toppings and sauces.

Freshly baked, still-warm pies, served with vanilla bean ice cream and drizzled with caramel sauce.

It's easy to dress up plain cakes and other desserts with chocolate leaves. Don't worry, I wouldn't even mention these garnishes if they were even a little difficult to make. Just brush some melted chocolate over a silk leaf. Chill on a plate in the fridge. When hard, peel the leaf away. No one has to know but you that you didn't craft those little delicacies with your own two hands.

Don't forget to have some sugar-free and low-fat selections around for your guests to enjoy.

"Don't Forgets"

Now for the "don't forgets!" In addition to ice, there are some minor, but oh so important, things you won't want to forget. And forget you won't (nor will anyone else) if you remember what I'm about to suggest! Have a Polaroid camera and a video camera on hand. Candid shots taken by guests using the disposable cameras you conspicuously placed throughout the party will usually produce the best mementos. Don't forget your standard camera — and make sure you have lots of extra film on hand. When you take the film in to be developed, ask for two prints. Your guests will appreciate copies (or . . . maybe not).

Hats are also a great party item. I'll address these in some plans but they can be used for any or all of them. The goofier the better. They're great icebreakers — instant mood enhancers. Masks, too. Picture your old Aunt Betty, the one who never cracks a smile, sporting reindeer antlers! (Bless her old heart — she probably won't discover them on her head for at least a week after your party!).

There you have it. You can close this book right now and have a party. However, it'll just happen, like so many others. So, please, keep reading — let's ice your cake.

Each plan contains ideas for a theme, invitations, decorations, menu, party favors, and attire. Keep The Cake in mind to carry out your theme. You'll find some extra tips in the plans. Remember, The Icing and The Cake are to be combined.

The Icing

You're now entering the danger zone. In the chapters to follow, you'll discover 71 truly unique holiday party ideas aching to jump off the pages into your life. Keep in mind that all's fair in love and war and in partying. The ideas were created with the spirit of the holidays first and foremost. I may hit a few buttons as I reveal my sense of humor, however, please don't be offended. Don't take this stuff too seriously. And if you do, you may need the ideas in this book far more than you'll ever know. And remember, for the health, safety, and general welfare of all concerned, temporarily disconnect your maturity, put your sense of humor on overdrive, whoop it up, kick back, and let loose. It's PARTY time!

Chapter 2

Charitable

The parties in this chapter are not only good-times-had-by-all get-togethers, but also, parties that allow your guests to do just that while at the same time selflessly indulging in the true meaning of Christmas. Guests are asked to do something at or bring something to your party to benefit a charity, a family shelter, children, the homeless, or some other community-based program that could use a little cheer. These are "Pause for a Cause" parties, where you and your guests take a little of your partying time (a "pause") to think about others who aren't as fortunate as you (a "cause"). Let's begin with a party that will brighten the holidays of some lesser-privileged children in your area.

Santa's Helpers: Workaholic Support Group

Here's a party for those worker-bees who have to keep on buzzing away no matter what the occasion. Life is work. Work is life. You've heard it all before. This party combines a great time with the project of collecting, wrapping, and delivering gifts to lesser-privileged children, surely to bring a smile to their adorable faces.

Invitations

Use small fabric elves. Do you remember those little elves that came wrapped around bars of soap at Christmas time? The ones with the felt body, plastic head, hands sewn together to embrace the bar of soap? That's what I have in mind. If you have no idea what I'm referring to (our mothers must not have bought the same soap) any 3-dimensional elf figure is fine, such as an ornament or other decoration. Write the party information on business card size pieces of paper and pin to the elves' hands to look as if they are holding little elf signs. Place the elf messengers in gift bags filled with straw, tie a ribbon around the handles, and hand-deliver. Another idea is to take packages of hot chocolate mix and cut sheets of paper the size of the package. Write the party information on the paper and attach it to the back of the envelope. Insert into another envelope and mail. The same idea can be used for single serving (or full) size boxes of Keebler® cookies. Make sure to ask your guests to bring an unwrapped child's gift. And make sure it's clear that your guests are going to work!

Attire

Efficient elf. Don pointy hats, pointy shoes, and pointy ears. How's that for getting to the point? No point in wasting any time.

Decorations

Set up your party in a garage, basement, attic, workshop, toolshed, or any other area that can be converted to Santa's workshop. Place a barber's pole at the entrance to the "workshop". If you don't have a barber's pole hanging around your house, you can easily make one by alternating red and white paint or paper onto a pole (existing lamp-post, pipe, or cardboard tubing will work). You'll know it's done right if it looks like a huge peppermint stick. Post a "North Pole" sign on it. Set up a large work table. This will be the hub of activity of the party. Arrange wrapping paper, bows, ribbon, scissors, and tape on the table. Put a train set on the middle of the table and let it chug-a-lug-a-choo-choo around and around. If the train cars are large enough, fill with candies, nuts, and whatever else will fit for your guests' nibbling pleasure as they busily wrap gifts. Play Christmas carols. And what would a workplace be without a boss snooping around, putting his two-cents in? Arrange for Santa to stop by to check on the progress (he is the boss after all).

Menu

Serve whatever a child loves to eat (no glue and crayons, please!) such as peanut butter and jelly sandwiches. Cut the bread with cookie cutters to form holiday shapes — wreaths and stars and stockings work best. Prepare grilled cheese, macaroni and cheese, hot dogs, and hamburgers. You could even make it real easy on yourself and order Happy Meals from the drive-thru window at your nearby McDonald's. Have lots of Keebler cookies and ice cold milk on hand, along with pitchers of Kool-Aid® (spike if you'd like). To satisfy the adult side of your guests, pour pitchers of Reindeer Milk and mugs of Mint Zingers.

Favors

I'm guessing that most of your guests probably didn't (couldn't, wouldn't) come through with the suggested attire (too busy, no doubt), so why don't you provide the get-up? If you're extremely patient and sort of creative, make elf shoes by sewing two pieces of felt together to form a sock that reaches about 5 inches above the ankle. Sew bells on the toes. A ribbon can be used to gather the "shoe" around the ankle. For a much easier, but equally fun version, use regular green socks (buy the extra-large size). Forget the pointed toes, but don't forget the bells — they can easily be sewn onto the sock. As your guests walk in, ask them to remove their shoes and put on the elf shoes. (Your next mission will be to convince your elves to put on those pointy ears you picked up at the Star Trek convention last year).

If a room full of elves with jingle bell shoes a-jingling and a-jangling will make you batty, or if you aren't a Trekkie and have no clue as to where to find those darn pointy ears (nor would you want to), why don't you try . . .

You Party Animal, You!

Throw a party for all your furry friends (pets, too)! Make it a time where you "paws for a cause".

Invitations

Invite your friends' and family members' pets by name and mention that its owner is also invited. If your human guests don't have a pet, let them bring their favorite stuffed toy animal or a neighbor's pet. Decorate some milk bones with red and green paint and attach rhinestones, glitter, sequins, and other festive items with a glue gun. Tie on a bow. Place in a box with shredded newspaper and party information. Or glue the party information on to the back of a box of milk bones and deliver. Ask your guests to bring pet treats and toys to donate to the Humane Society or local animal shelter.

Attire

Fur, real or faux. Collars and leashes are optional for human guests.

Decorations

This party is ideally held outdoors (for obvious reasons), so if weather permits, set it up outside. Place plastic fire hydrants, trimmed with tinsel and lights, around the yard, patio, or other party area.

Decorate all indoor and outdoor trees with lights and milk bones. Use sheets of newspaper to cover serving tables, countertops, and floors. 101 Dalmatian items have flooded the market — you should be able to find all kinds of plates, napkins, and decorations that you can holiday-ize.

Menu

Serve any of the Cake suggestions in dog bowls (buy brand new bowls and leave the price tags on to reassure your guests!) Buy or bake cookies shaped like dogs and other animals, bones, paw prints, and mailmen. How about a bone-shaped cake? Place bowls of sunflower seeds down for the bird lovers on your list. Spicy hot chili is always a favorite (and, in keeping with the theme, it looks like dog food. I know! I know! Perhaps I've gone a bit too far. But you must admit that after the initial reaction wears off, it's not such a bad idea!).

Favors

Choose squeaky Christmas toys and balls for your furry guests (for the pets, too). Set out rawhide chewies. There are figurines and note cards representing all breeds — your guests might enjoy one with their animal featured. Then there are dog collars or jars of human "milk bones" (cookies shaped like bones in case you're wondering).

If the outdoors are out and you just put down new carpet, why don't you try . . .

Presents Are Present

Your guests bring wrapped gifts that will make a difference to a child this holiday season.

Invitations

Put the party information on a beautiful sheet of paper and wrap it in the biggest box you can find and manage. Fill with shredded tissue paper and silver tinsel. Gift wrap and deliver. Ask your guests to bring a wrapped gift for a lesser-privileged child, noting whether the gift is for a boy or a girl and for what age group.

Attire

Giftwear. (Not to be confused with "giftware" however, you may very well start the next trend if you run with this).

Decorations

General Christmas with lots of presents present. Wrap, ribbon, and bow as many empty boxes of all shapes and sizes and place all over the party area. You could also gift wrap anything in a box form in the party area such as doors (including cabinet doors), bathroom vanities, the refrigerator, wall hangings, mirrors, and so on. Wrap your serving table like a huge gift. Run a strip of large ribbon down the length and across the width of the table. Place a gigantic bow in the center of the table and thread greenery through the loops and place ornaments around it. Secure all with safety and straight pins, or a hot glue gun. Place serving pieces on top of wrapped boxes of assorted sizes and stacked at various heights. Use the same paper for all the boxes; for example, use all gold foil paper with red velvet ribbons or all green metallic with red plaid ribbons. For unique serving pieces, wrap box bottoms and tops separately in Christmas paper. Line the bottom portions of the box and fill with food. Lean the lids against the bottoms. Use tape to secure. The look you are trying to achieve is delicious food gleaming from just opened gift boxes, allowing your guests to not only sneak a peek at the delicious gastronomical gift, but leaving enough of an opening to allow your guests to grab whatever treats are being offered. Thread lights and ribbons and bows around the table to finish the look.

Menu

General Christmas. Bricks of cream cheese, rounds of brie, loaves of bread, and squares of cake make tasty packages. Gift wrap these foods using "edible ribbons" such as pimento strips, carrot curls, and licorice strings and sticks.

Favors

Any present, beautifully wrapped will delight your guests. Give books on how-to gift wrap with individuality with a spool of festive ribbon.

If the thought of wrapping one more gift box has you running for cover, why don't you try . . .

Kid Wanna-bes: No Kidding!

This is a kids only party where only adults are invited. Yes, you read right. I'm talking about all those adults who are children at times by choice, or all the time for those who just can't help themselves. To decipher the wanna-be code, you need to take reality and manipulate it a bit. For example, if one of your guests is 47 years old, add four plus seven to get eleven. Your guest is a wanna-be eleven year-old for party purposes. You and your guests will take a trip to a local hospital to drop off some gifts to the children who are in the hospital during the holidays. They'll love the attention, the gifts, the sights (you and your guests' clown/children clothes).

Invitations

Use store-bought juvenile invitations or make them yourself (just don't be delinquent). A Christmas theme coloring book with the party information stapled to the cover and a box of crayons is a clever way to let your guests know you're having a party. Ask your guests to bring a wrapped gift for a child, one that is suitable for either a boy or a girl. (Mention that games are the best choices because a number of children can share them).

Attire

Christmas clownish or childish, or both.

Decorations

Anything you'd do for a child's party. Make sure you have lots of balloons, streamers, paper chains, and children size hats, plates, and utensils. Serve food in toys, for example, a dump truck full of pretzels or a Barbie® convertible or swimming pool full of chips and dip. Scatter red and green crayons with Christmas confetti across the serving table. Play pin the nose on Rudolph, or pin the nose on Frosty the Snowman, or pin all sorts of things on Santa.

Menu

Same as Santa's Helpers: Workaholic Support Group party. Serve anything children love to eat.

Favors

Have prizes for the most childlike attire and game winners. Hand out Matchbox® cars, Barbie dolls, or all-time favorites such as Legos® and Lincoln Logs®.

If you don't wanna-be anything but outta the holiday season, why don't you try . . .

How the Grinch Tried to Steal Christmas

The idea for this party came from my favorite holiday classic *How the Grinch Stole Christmas* by Dr. Suess. Thanks to my friend Betsy, I no longer have to calendar the broadcast of this hit in my Filofax. I now have my own video to watch whenever I please (which usually happens in the wee hours of the morning when the rest of the eastern standard time country is sound asleep). This party is about the Grinch's failure to steal Christmas. Oh, he tried, I'll give him that, but his scheme didn't quite go as planned. In the original version, he stole a number of items from the residents of Whoville. Here's what he took from those poor folks: Stockings all hung in a row, pop guns, bicycles, roller skates, drums, checkerboards, tricycles, popcorn, plums, who-pudding, roast beast, the last can of who-hash, the Christmas tree, and the log for the fire. The goal of your party is to have your guests round up the items he took (they are to bring them to the party) and return Christmas to Whoville which, for the purposes of this party is a family shelter, a children's hospital, or a fire or police department that is coordinating a gift drive for children. In the end, all the goodies will be returned to the sweet children of Whoville. A merry holiday after all thanks to you and your guests.

Invitations

The party information could be attached to the cover of the book by Dr. Suess and mailed to each guest (at book rate). Explain what the purpose of the party is (it's always a blast to purposefully party) and provide a list of things to bring.

Attire

Dr. Suess-ish. If you have a cat in your hat, you're already ahead of the game!

Decorations

This is where it gets really creative. Whoville is the place to be and therein lies the challenge. Look through the pages of Dr. Suess's book. For the most part, your General Christmas will do, however there may be some touches that will make Whoville that special place it is. After all the "stolen" items have been captured and bagged for return to the happy children of Whoville, the celebration begins. Have a special showing of the movie with lots of popcorn.

Menu

General Christmas. Make sure to include plums, who-pudding, roast beast, and the last can of who-hash.

Favors

Send your guests home with a video of the movie or at least a case of who-hash (make labels to paste over the labels on cans of corned beef hash). Candies in a gift bag with "thank you" notes from the children of Whoville for making their Christmas special make for a great favor.

If you still haven't recovered from the green eggs and ham served at the last Dr. Suess party you crashed, why don't you try . . .

We Wish You a Beary Christmas

Everyone brings a teddy bear to this slumber party (sort of like a date, and a sleepover one at that). The bears will then be donated to a children's hospital, shelter, or local fire or police department.

Invitations

Tiny teddy bears with the party information rolled to fit in the bears' arms in a bag filled with straw. Or, wrap the party information around a Sue Bee® honey container (the cute little plastic, squeeze-bottle bear filled with honey). Pieces of paper cut out in shapes of teddy bears with the party information printed on it will also work. Tell your guests they're invited to a slumber party (they don't have to stay over, but they could if space permits or they have to!) — you could go right into Not a Pretty Sight: The Morning After party and serve those Bloody Marys.

Attire

Seasonal slumber: Footed pajamas with a convenient flap in the back and nightshirts with nightcaps (or is it a nightshirt after a night-cap?) Other kinds of teddies are okay, if you dare. Sleeping bags are optional. Remind your guests not to forget to bring any special pillow or blankie they must have to get a decent night's sleep.

Decorations

Any bear stuff will do but there's nothing like Pooh. Winnie-the-Pooh in rare holiday form is where it's at. There are so many Pooh products out there these days — you'll be able to pick up plates, cups, napkins, and tablecloths adorned with this adorable little bear. If you have a bear collection, dress them up in tiny Santa caps (or big ones for big bears) and holiday garb. Tie red bows around their necks (please, not too tight). Seat them around the party area so they can mingle with your guests. Place fluffy bed pillows on the chairs, couch, and the floor in the party area. Bring out any quilts you have. Try to create that slumber party feel. Show a holiday movie such as Tim Allen's, *Santa Clause*.

Menu

Slumber party noshes (any of the General Christmas quick fixes). Serve popcorn and punch by the bowlful. Treat your guests to honey buns and Honey Browns® (a tasty beer). Have an assortment of pizzas delivered. Make sure you have plenty of BearBeer on hand (remember, you can call anything you want to call it, so pick up a case of generic beer and rename accordingly). Serve anything with "bearies" on it, you know, strawbearies, bluebearies, cranbearies, and dinglebearies.

Favors

Your guests will enjoy holiday jars topped with a square of holiday fabric and tied with kitchen string filled with homemade honey mustard. Other treats include *Winnie-the-Pooh* books (there are so many make-you-smile ones out there) and teddy bear ornaments.

If you can't "bear" another "bearly" there get-together, or you think this plan is nothing more than the same old pooh, why don't you try . . .

Silent Night, Holey Night

No, that's not a typo. It's supposed to be "holey", as in full of holes. This party features a silent auction and another challenge. The auction benefits a charity of your choice (discuss your plans with the charity to make sure all is in order — especially important if you're soliciting donors of goods and services for the auction) and the challenge is creating a menu of "holey" foods. Before the party, collect gift certificates for goods and services such as spa packages including manicures, pedicures, facials, and a massage; car washes and waxes; lunch for two; and a weekend away for your guests to bid on.

Invitations

Send bid cards (attach a 6-inch square piece of poster board to a popsicle stick and write a number on it) to your guests with the party information on the backside of the card. Include a list of what will be available with suggested minimum bids. Let them know who the beneficiary is (and no . . . it really shouldn't be you!)

Attire

Holey clothes.

Decorations

General Christmas. Arrange the auction table attractively. Place the items to be bid on mountains of snow. (*See* Ski Bunnies — Oops! Wrong Holiday, I Mean Ski Funnies — Aprés Ski Wheeeee! and Let It Snow! Let It Snow! And . . . Let It Snow! parties for snow ideas.)

Menu

For starters, why not serve some Swiss cheese and crackers? This snack minimally satisfies the "holey something" requirement. Other ideas include tortellini with sauce and parmesan cheese. Miniature bagel bites topped with pasta sauce, shredded mozzarella cheese, and sliced black olives are delicious. Dessert is easy. Serve bundt cake (the big hole) and angel food cake (the big holy hole), and, yes, even doughnuts. Chic restaurant patrons are really getting in to glamorizing the once-for-cops-only rings of dough. Doughnuts are being offered after dinner in all the really cool restaurants in the big cities. Be cool, too. Serve the holes! Offer plain cake doughnuts with bowls and tubes of assorted frostings and sprinkles such as shredded coconut, grated chocolate, nonpareils, silver dragees, and powdered and granulated sugar. Your guests can make 'em like they love 'em.

Favors

Wrap the silent auction items in seasonal tissue paper and place in a holiday gift bag topped with shredded tissue and Christmas potpourri in cinnamon, spice, or pine.

If you can't keep silent when you think of what (or who) comes to mind when you're talking about the center of a doughnut, why don't you try . . .

The Twelve Nights of Christmas

This is the crime-riddled evil stepsister of the traditional Twelve Days of Christmas. You know how it usually goes: 12 drummers drumming, 11 pipers piping, 10 lords-a-leaping, 9 ladies dancing, 8 maids-a-milking, 7 swans-a-swimming, 6 geese-a-laying, 5 golden rrrrrrrrings!, 4 calling birds, 3 French hens, 2 turtle doves, and a partridge in a pear tree. Well, I've changed this a bit. The Twelve Nights of Christmas involve the following "activities": 12 rummers driving, 11 snipers sniping, 10 lords-a-looting, 9 burglars prowling, 8 meter maids-a-ticketing, 7 cashiers a-skimming, 6 cops-high-speed-chasing, 5 stolen rrrrrrrrings,! 4 jail birds, 3 hench men, 2 burly thugs, and a cartridge in an artery. True, this party isn't as upbeat as its beautiful stepsister. In fact, it's quite ugly. I know I promised fantasies and fun, not "murder and mayhem" as my husband likes to call this particular party. My feeling is this: Crime is real and unfortunately it is non-discriminatory. It doesn't hold off until the holidays are over before it rears its ugly head. Bad things happen to good people and if this party could bring generous people together to help ease the pain of those less fortunate, it's a great party! To this end, ask your guests to bring care packages full of non-perishable foods, personal hygiene products, and gently worn clothing to be given to people displaced from their homes or to victims of crime who need help.

*I*nvitations

Subpoena your guests to appear. Your invitation can read something like this:

IN THE TOWN OF PALM
BEACH, IN AND FOR
PALM BEACH COUNTY
Case No. X-Mas 12-25

In Re: Holiday Cheer

_____/

SUBPOENA FOR PARTY

The State of Florida
To: (your guest's name)

> You are hereby commanded to appear at the Smith's residence, 32 Oak Street, Palm Beach, Florida, on the ____ day of December, 19__, at 8:00 P.M. for the taking of your holiday pulse and temperature. If you fail to appear, your name will be deleted from Santa's good boys and girls list. Expect coal.

> You are further commanded to bring with you one care package to be given to a person in need. If you fail to do so, expect a double dose of coal.

WITNESS my hand and seal on this ____ day of December, 19__.

The Smith's

*A*ttire

Jailbird garb. Black and white stripes. Ball and chain are optional.

Decorations

General Christmas. Invite a local Karate Kid to demonstrate a few self defense techniques. (Ask the Kid if he or she would wear their green belt instead of their black one to your party to fit in with the decor).

Menu

Jailhouse slop. You know, the awful food they serve in prison such as prime rib, filet mignon, baked potatoes, fresh vegetables, soup du jour, chocolate-swirl cheesecake, and lots of bread and water. Set up the buffet like a prison food line (I know, chances are you've never seen one — it's like a school cafeteria line). Stack cheap plastic trays, paper plates and napkins, and utensils (make sure all knives are dull) at the beginning of the line.

Favors

Wrap self defense handbooks with black and white striped paper. Pass out coupons for a karate or kick-boxing class. Place pepper spray, mace, whistles, and other self protection products in a holiday bag.

If you are barred from having this party or think it's an absolute crime to throw it during the holidays, or if your in-house arrest ankle bracelet will alert headquarters if you try to walk your guests to their cars at the end of the evening, why don't you try . . .

Box Me, Tip Me, Make Me Do Stupid Things

This party was inspired by Boxing Day, an English holiday held on December 26th. It's called "Boxing Day" after the alms boxes located in churches that were broken open so their contents could be distributed to the poor. Later, it became a day on which one would tip servants, shop assistants, and other helpers. Now, it's a day to relax and have a wonderful time. So, let your guests relax while you serve them and they tip you. The idea is similar to the Leukemia Society's Celebrity Waiter fund-raiser, where "important" people are assigned a table to wait on. The deal is that the waiter doesn't do a thing unless he or she is given a tip, preferably a big fat one. Want a glass of water? Pay me. Oh, you want a spoon for your soup? Pay me. Imitate Cuba Gooding Jr. and Tom Cruise in the movie *Jerry Maguire* as they repeatedly stated, "Show me the money!" All the tips you receive will go to charity. Contact the Leukemia Society for assistance — let them know what you're thinking and work together.

Invitations

Boxes within boxes. Find three different size boxes that you'll be able to nest inside each other. Take the smallest one and place the party information in it and toss in some Christmas potpourri and shredded "money" (play money cut in thin strips). Wrap in brown paper and tie with twine. Place inside the next box and wrap it up. Place this one in the largest box and wrap. Include instructions to your guests that you'll be performing for money (Free legal advice: Be very careful how you word and work this — there are some things you can't do for money!)

Attire

Charitable chic. Wear boxer shorts and boxing gloves. Walk softly and carry a big wallet.

Decorations

General Christmas. This is an ideal party to hold in a restaurant. Your charitable mission will be accomplished with someone else getting stuck with the set up and clean up.

Menu

General Christmas or restaurant menu.

Favors

Hand out maid-for-a-day coupons or restaurant two-for-one certificates. Wrap pretty boxes for keepsakes or jewelry. Have boxer shorts silk-screened across the seat: "I boxed it at the Smith's".

If the only boxing you are into has something to do with the famous boxing promoter, Don King (his hair alone could be the subject of a party and a wild one at that), why don't you try . . .

Chapter ☀ 3

Sports

These parties are for all the sports fanatics out there who won't come up for air long enough to celebrate the holidays. So, the holidays have to be brought to them. Your guests will enjoy glowing like Rudolph the red-nosed reindeer if you decide to tackle any (or all) of the football bowl parties. Or, send your guests down a slippery slope, or simply get them teed-off. You'll score a lot of points hosting these spirited events.

Reindeer Glow Bowl

Starring Rudolph the Red-Nosed Quarterback. A close of the football season reason (yet another excuse) to party holiday-style. (Author's comment: Of course, the close of any football season is grounds for a celebration — no excuses needed).

Invitations

Write the party information on small footballs with a gold or silver metallic pen. Place the ball in a sports-theme gift bag, fill with shredded astro-turf green tissue paper, and hand-deliver. Another idea is to have beer bottle labels printed with the party information and place on beer bottles over the original labels. Put the bottles in brown paper bags, fill with some astro-turf green paper, twist and secure the top with a red ribbon, and deliver. Or, you could staple a sheet of paper that has the party information printed on it to the back of a bag of beer nuts or cherry drops (Rudolph's nose — get it?), and deliver.

Attire

Holiday cheery (cherry) wear: Put on your favorite team jerseys, caps, helmets, cheerleader outfits, pompoms, and red glowing noses.

Decorations

Make your party area look and feel like a sports bar. Hang football team banners, pennants, and posters. Find a few guys who've had a few beers to hang out in front of your television, preferably set up near a bar, with bottles of Budweiser® in their hands, eyes mindlessly gazing at a television screen featuring men grabbing, slapping, and falling all over each other. Use football-shaped serving pieces. These can be picked up at a party supply store, as can other football party items. Football helmets can also be put to good use. Use them to hold utensils, napkins, bread, and dry snacks. Put astro-turf on the serving table and other surfaces — kitchen countertops and bar tops. And, what's a reindeer bowl without the reindeer? Place stuffed-toy and plastic blow-up reindeer dressed in team garb throughout the party area . . . make sure one has a red nose!

Menu

Think tailgates. Serve a variety of sausage and salami logs, bricks of cheese, and crocks of mustards. Use a large wood cutting board as the serving piece for the logs, bricks, and crocks. Fill baskets with assorted breads — loaves (thickly and thinly sliced) and rolls of rye, multi-grain, sour Dasher and Dancer dough, and old-fashioned white. Creatively arrange (in the shape of a Christmas tree) Cupid cold cuts and cheese slices, tomato and onion slices, and lettuce leaves on platters. Fill bowls with pickles (slices and chips), olives, and hot peppers. Serve Prancer potato salad, cole slaw, Blitzen baked beans, and other side dishes. Delight your guests with beer-steamed hot dogs and soft pretzels, Comet chips, dips, nuts, and other munchies, and Buffalo chicken wings, celery stalks, and blue cheese Donner dressing. Throw in some Vixen vittles. You get the picture. As for beverages, serve Rudolph "reinbeer" (regular beer labeled especially for you). Or, attach a large label to the side of a keg. Don't forget root beer and Reindeer Milk. For the sweet tooth, score a touchdown with brownies and cookies — chocolate chip and sugar with team color icing. Bowls of those cherry drops and chocolate covered raisins and peanuts (Rudolph noses and reindeer "droppings") will help create the atmosphere.

Favors

Tickets to local sporting events will score big. Toss some Nerf™ footballs and team paraphernalia to your guests as they leave. Offer antlers to your guests (pet shops sell these during the holidays — they'll work on most humans). Toast your guests with beer steins filled with beer nuts and wrapped in cellophane squares, with the ends brought together at the top and tied with team color ribbons.

*E*xtras

Here are some special suggestions for "real" bowl games Rudolph is known to crash on January 1st each year.

Sugar Bowl

Invitations: Buy some sugar packets like the kind you find in a restaurant. Print the party information on separate pieces of paper the size of the sugar packet. For example, put each one of the following messages on the back of a packet of sugar: "You are invited", "to a Sugar Bowl", "Party", "January 1st at noon", "The Smith's — 110 Main", "R.S.V.P. 555-1212 by December 27th". Mix the six printed packets with a few plain packets in a Christmas motif bowl with some shredded white tissue paper or straw. Place in a box and deliver. Your guests will wonder what the heck they've received — when they notice the first message they'll start to figure it out.

Orange Bowl

Invitations: Place an orange in a wood crate with green straw, team colors, and the party information.

Rose Bowl

Invitations: One long stem rose with the party information and a tiny football charm or referee whistle tied to it with ribbons in team colors.

Fiesta Bowl

Check out Fiesta, Then Siesta party for ideas.

If you don't think you'll score with this one, why don't you try . . .

Ski Bunnies — Oops! Wrong Holiday, I Mean Ski Funnies — Aprés Ski WHEEEEE!

This is a great party to have after a ski trip. Invite friends over to look at photos, videos, casts, and assorted bumps and bruises.

Invitations

Place Santa caps on little stuffed animal bunnies (crutches optional) holding party information and placed in a little basket filled with shredded comic pages (the funnies) from the newspaper, and a tiny bottle of Peppermint Schnapps. Cover the shredded comics with fake snow. If using a printed invitation, put some fake snow and confetti cut in the shape of little bunnies in the envelope before sealing. Another suggestion is to recreate a lift ticket with your party site as the mountain. For example, "Smith's Snowmess Mountain" with the party information printed on it.

Attire

Funny bunny aprés skiwear. Throw on those sweaters, slacks, boots, mittens, gloves, ski caps, and rabbit ears.

Decorations

You'll want to transform the party area into a ski lodge. If you have a fireplace, you're almost there. If you don't, turn your television into one. Buy or rent a videotape that shows a roaring fire on the screen (check with your video rental store). Hang a moose head above the mantle and your guests will feel as if they've miraculously and magically landed in Aspen. Put twinkling white lights on all indoor plants and trees. Hang snowflake cutouts from fishing line throughout the party area. Build snow drifts at your entranceway. Place cardboard boxes around the area at different heights, cover them with sheets of white cotton and then sprinkle or spray artificial snow all over it. To really make it special, place a string of white lights under the cotton for a beautiful glow (battery or plug-in depending on where the nearest electrical outlet is). Line your walkway with luminaries. (*See* The Cake.) Do the same on your serving table. Stack sturdy boxes of various sizes on the table, cover with cotton, lights, and fake snow. Make slopes. Put serving pieces on top of different boxes so the food is at different levels. Place miniature Christmas trees around the mountains. An ice sculpture would really finish this scene off.

Menu

Grill wild game if it's available — buffalo, elk, caribou, venison. Serve a wild mushroom soup and crispy fried potatoes. Buy some Hostess Snowballs® (chocolate cupcake mounds rolled in coconut) or make your own coconut "snow" cake (frost a white cake with vanilla frosting and dust with coconut flakes). Pour *Fran's Reindeer Milk* and the various hot chocolate and Schnapps' drinks. (*See* Chapter One for recipes.) Make oyster shooters (popular at ski resorts). Put an oyster in a shot glass, bathe in tequila, and dab with horseradish or cocktail sauce. Swallow quickly (very).

Favors

Hand out personalized ski caps, gift certificates or coupons for a discount at a ski shop, and a rabbit's foot for good luck.

If the only white you think of when you see the word "ski" is the body cast you wore after your first downhill (head first) run, why don't you try . . .

Teed-Off Golf Gala

A good round of golf is very difficult, if not impossible, when it snows. Have you ever tried to find that little white ball in a snow bank? And that neon orange ball they designed for snow golfing is no better. And those extra long tees you have to use are a royal pain in the ace.

So, before you trade in your sand rake for a snow shovel, I have a good idea. Why not throw this party as a way to weather the winter until it's safe to come out and play? You're teed off because you're not on the green, however there could be worse things. (You could be a person who's just teed-off all the time). For now, enjoy your time on the 19th hole. Think positive!

Invitations

A printed invitation stuffed in an envelope with a few red and green tees. Or, a sleeve of golf balls with the party information attached, asking your guests to come on over and have a ball, especially since there's nothing else to do when the courses are closed.

Attire

Festivi-tee golf garb. Put on some Paine Stewart knickers (how painful) and Foot Joy spikes (could be equally painful — how joyous can a spiked foot be?).

Decorations

General Christmas with an extra dose of green. Turn the party area into the 19th hole (it's the only hope you have). Lean a few golf bags against the wall, full of clubs decorated with garland, ribbons, and bows. Of course (golf course that is) invite a golfing Santa decked out in red knickers, a white polo shirt, red golf sweater, and the same old hat he always wears to your party. He can arrive in a decorated-for-the-holidays golf cart and hand out party favors from the golf bag he has slung over his shoulder. For fun, watch a golf tournament on TV or pop in a golf-tip video. Set up an indoor putting green and have a contest.

Menu

General Christmas with a 19th hole full bar. Rename a popular shooter for the occasion. How about calling melon balls "Ace Shots"? Little green shooters that go right in the hole (your mouth). Everybody does some "Ace shots" and they wish they really could. Serve some

"Irons and woods" (liver paté and crackers served on a wood tray). Don't forget the big birdie (a huge turkey, roasted, and sliced all over the place). Serve lots of Chili dip with corn chips (better do a few more shots at this time!) and Bogie bean dip with tortilla triangles. Don't forget beef, veal, or lamb shanks. Anything par for the course is a sure thing.

Favors

Present balls, tees, golf towels, and certificates for a golf lesson or a round of golf to your guests.

If it would be too frustrating to just sit around talking about golf, though admittedly, not as frustrating as actually playing the game, why don't you try . . .

Chapter ☀4

Ladies ☆Only

First of all, let me make it clear that these parties aren't really for ladies only. Gentlemen are also invited. However, I have four brothers and lots of male friends and I haven't found one yet that has gotten really excited about psychics, a cup of tea, shopping, and other ideas of fun my girlfriends and I have in mind. Having said that, the eight parties you'll find in this chapter are great escapes for you and your friends (of whatever gender) to kick back and unwind during the more often than not harried holiday season.

Get De-Stressed!

Feeling a little stressed? Who ya gonna call? Stress-Busters! That's what this party is all about — busting holiday stress.

Invitations

Tie a piece of paper with the party information on it to a toy hammer or mallet or a pair of tiny boxing gloves. Or, fill pill bottles with candy "pills" with the party information on the prescription label. Deliver in a box or a bag filled with shredded black paper.

Attire

The most casual you've ever been. No make-up. No fancy hair. Wrinkled clothes are okay. Roll out of bed and come on over! No stress dressing.

Decorations

General Christmas with piñatas. Piñatas are colorful, tissue-paper covered hollow objects that can be filled with candy and small trinkets which are released when the piñata is split open. Hang a few holiday piñatas in an area large enough to accommodate adults swinging big sticks. Your guests are given a stick, blindfolded, spun around a few times, and told to take their best shot in busting stress. Put "Knock Out Stress" signs on the piñatas to use as targets. Hire a massage therapist to treat your guests to a quick, but oh-so-needed, neck and shoulder rub.

Menu

Did you know that stressed spelled backwards is DESSERTS?!! And did you know that the numero uno comfort food is chocolate? So, you offer chocolate, and lots of it in all shapes, sizes, and forms.

Favors

Pass out gift books on stress management or gift certificates for a massage. Another fun idea is to give stress bags to squeeze when stress surfaces! (Fill deflated balloons with sand and knot the end closed). Scented candles will also delight your guests.

If a room full of blindfolded, stressed out people carrying big sticks doesn't sound like a way to eliminate stress, why don't you try . . .

Candy Canes: Christmas Crutches

A little holiday assistance.

Invitations

Print your party information on a sheet of 8-inch x 8-inch plain white paper using red ink. Wrap the sheet around an extra large candy cane or peppermint stick. Secure the invitation with a tiny piece of tape and finish off with a festive ribbon and bow. Hand-deliver or mail in a tube filled with shredded white and red tissue paper and red sparkles.

Attire

Anything red and white (preferably striped) is right.

Decorations

Naturally, your primary colors will be red and white (what an idea!). Replace your regular light bulbs with red bulbs. Use red and white napkins and red and white plastic utensils. Mix the two colors (red fork, white spoon, red knife, for example) and roll utensils in a red napkin and a white napkin placed on top of each other. Insert a candy cane and tie with a red and white striped ribbon. Place the utensil "bundles" in a natural colored basket. Since there are so many shades of red, I'd suggest using white for the larger background items, such as the tablecloth, and buy the accent items in red.

Menu

You guessed it . . . red and white food. A pasta bar works nicely here — serve marinara and white clam sauce with a variety of pasta. I've seen Christmas tree shaped pasta for sale in delicatessen and specialty shops. To satisfy the sweet tooth, whip up a batch of candy cane cookies. Use cookie cutters on sugar cookie dough and decorate with red and white icing, after baking according to directions. Or try these: Take sugar cookie dough (mix from a favorite recipe or buy already prepared in dairy section) and divide in half. Add red food coloring to one half. Roll dough into strips. Twist red and white strips together and form into candy cane shapes. Bake per directions. Sprinkle with red sugar crystals while still hot. Of course, in the spirit of this theme, place real candy canes and more candy canes and peppermint candies in every size and shape you can find in a variety of containers — glass or crystal jars, baskets, and china or pottery bowls. For a special beverage, serve Mint Zingers in thick mugs.

Favors

You could hold a best/worst candy cane contest judging your guests in their theme attire. The winners would receive canes with gift certificates attached. First prize (large cane), second prize (medium cane), and third prize (you guessed it, the smallest cane you can find). Party favors include anything peppermint (bath stuff, foot lotion, Schnapps, or after dinner mints).

If red and white leaves you blue, why don't you try . . .

Prediction: You Will Attend an Awesome Party

A new year. Perhaps a new you? If only you knew! Ah . . . but you can know. Mingle with psychic movers and shakers and catch a glimpse of what's to come in the year ahead.

Invitations

Staple a tea bag to the invitation and put in a "crystal ball" clear envelope, inviting your friends to take a peek into the future to find out what the year ahead has in store for them. Or do a palm invitation: Trace your hand on sturdy paper and cut out, writing the party information along the lines of the palm. Ask your guests to let you know what their astrological sign is (or the date of their birth) when they R.S.V.P.

Attire

Futuristic or Santa gypsy. Wear crystal jewelry and glad rags.

Decorations

You want to create the feeling of Mardi Gras in December. I'm not thinking of voodoo dolls with cute little Santa hats, but you can! Hook up with some astrologers, palm readers, fortune-tellers, and gypsies. Set up tables with crystal balls, tarot cards, and tea leaves for the clairvoyants you hired to set your guests on the right paths. Make sure you have lots of candles and incense. You want to create an aura of mystique — an atmosphere that will attract the spirits. (Liquid spirits will do the trick).

Menu

General Christmas with a Cajun twist — some crawfish, red beans and rice, and jambalaya. Offer assorted teas and Vodka Voodoo Punch (vodka mixed with anything capable of a punch).

Favors

Buy each of your guests a horoscope book filled with predictions for the upcoming year. Give boxes of tea. Other ideas include a rose quartz crystal (brings love), a bay candle to be lit on New Year's Day for good fortune, tarot cards, runes, or Ouija boards.

If you predict that this party isn't where it's at, and you're crystal clear on that prediction, why don't you try . . .

Falalalalala . . . Ahhh . . . Spa

A party for all the goddesses and princesses you know.

Invitations

Re-label a bottle of bubble bath with the party information. Or, put the information in a gift bag with a loofah and a pine-needle scented shower gel. Peppermint body/foot lotion or scrub is a seasonal idea — add a candy cane or two. Include the brochure of the spa you've selected. Check around — chances are good that there's a day spa in your area, making pampering moments accessible to everyone. (Budget tip: As the hostess of this party, don't feel that you have to pay for everyone's treatments — your role is coordinator. Ask your friends what services they'd like and make the appointments. Include confirmations and prices in their invite/gift bags).

Attire

Seasonsational spa smocks. Don't even consider anything with belts, buckles, or buttons. Go for what you can pullover or pull up for the most comfort.

Decorations

General Christmas is enough. Everyone can meet at your house before heading over to the spa. Have classical carols playing in the background and spice scented candles saturating the air with a relaxing aroma.

Menu

Serve mimosas, bagels, and fruit before your adventure. Return to your house after the day of bliss for some more champagne and some wine and cheese with crackers and fruit. Sit around and talk about how you don't want the day to end.

Favors

Surprise your friends with some memento of your day. Check out the gift shop at the spa and pick up a little something for your spa pals

. . . a visor or baseball cap, a T-shirt or a tank top, or other item imprinted with the spa's logo. You can put together a nice take-home-remember-this-day gift bag with these items or other products including anything for the bath and candles. Sprinkle with potpourri or rose petals before handing over to your friends.

If you feel you'll take a soak on this one, why don't you try . . .

A Message To Santa: Lighten Up!

This party is a nice break from the high-fat fare thrown at us from all directions. This is a holiday-calming opportunity. You and your guests will have a detoxifying grand time.

Invitations

Staple the party information to a bag of pretzels. Or tie a bunch of carrots with some raffia, tuck in a sprig of holly and the party information, and place in a brown bag. A bunch of fragrant herbs will also do the trick, as will a clove studded orange nested in a straw-filled box. A fruit basket also makes a delicious invitation.

Attire

Festive action. Warm-up and jogging suits, workout clothes, sweatshirts and pants, sneakers and tube socks, and baseball caps and sweatbands are appropriate.

Decorations

General Christmas. Invite an emaciated Santa to greet your guests and hand out party favors. Dust off your gym equipment and use as props. For example, wrap dumb bells with garland and put on the serving table. Use a step on a table as a serving pad. Pop in Joanie Greggains', *Holiday Workout* in your VCR to get some aerobic conditioning steps all performed with your favorite Christmas songs in the background. Turn fruit into candle holders. Cut the tops off some oranges and apples and scoop out enough flesh to hold a votive or taper candle (the tighter the better). Make sure the bottom of the fruit is even to keep the candle upright. If it isn't, cut the bottom evenly across to stabilize it. Arrange on branches placed across the table. A raw veggie tree placed in the middle of your serving table makes a deliciously pleasing centerpiece (directions below).

Menu

Set up a salad bar with a selection of fat-free dressings. Hand out bags of air-popped or low-fat microwave popcorn. Offer warm soft pretzels with mustard and reduced fat crackers and cheese. Have a platter of fruit chunks to dunk in no-fat fudge sauce, raspberry sauce, no-fat caramel, even marshmallow fluff (remember that stuff? Yum!) Firm fruits such as pineapple, apples, strawberries, pears, and bananas are the best dunkers. Arrange raw vegetables on trays with bowls of no-fat dressings. Make a veggie tree to use as an edible centerpiece. Cover a Styrofoam™ cone with herbs (pin or use a hot glue gun). Put an assortment of raw veggies on toothpicks and stick into the herb tree as decorations. Have veggie dips nearby. This also works with fruit and complimentary dips. Arrange cold platters of reduced fat cheese slices with rolled slices of lean meats and poultry, a variety of mustards, and no-fat mayonaise. Healthy eating doesn't mean you can't enjoy dessert. In fact, it's unhealthy to think you can never enjoy sweets. Offer candy canes (sugar, yes, but no fat), Rice Krispies® marshmallow treats, and an assortment of Snackwell® products — candies, cookies, cakes or other no-fat/reduced fat snacks. Serve fat-free hot chocolate topped with marshmallows, fresh fruit juices and herbal teas served with honey sticks. Have on hand assorted bottled waters with lemon, lime, and orange slices to garnish.

Favors

Hand out passes to a local gym. Bag a workout video and a pair of new shoelaces (Christmas green or red). Fill a water bottle imprinted with the party information with healthy stuff such as sugar-free gum and candies (peppermint or wintergreen), a packet of bath oil to soothe overworked muscles, and pretzels. Offer tank tops or T-shirts imprinted with the party information on it.

If this makes no sense before January 1st, why don't you try . . .

Plump It, Don't Pump It!: Santa's Diet Support Group

This is an all-out binge party. What more can I say?

Invitations

Attach the party information to a string tied to a red helium balloon decorated to look like a Santa ready to explode (you can buy these balloons at a party supply store). Hand-deliver to your guests.

Attire

Hungry togs with expandable waistbands.

Decorations

General Christmas with a Santa-style workout area. Don't fret. All you need is a VCR, a TV, and some comfortable chairs and tables to put the food on (large tables for lots of food). Arrange food on bathroom, kitchen, and postal scales. Borrow them from your family, friends, neighbors, and from people you don't even know or like. "Workout" by watching Richard Simmons exercise videos. Load up on buttered popcorn, Raisinets®, and Whoppers®. Don't be shy and I'm telling you why, Santa Claus is coming to town! And he's hungry!

Menu

No fat gram counting here! Anything goes! This is a feeding frenzy of binge favorites.

*F*avors

Stuff a fat gram counter book in to a Santa cap. A copy of Santa's tried and true diet plan will bring a smile to your guests' faces:

> *Breakfast:* $\frac{1}{2}$ grapefruit and a cup of coffee. *Mid-morning Snack:* $\frac{1}{4}$ of a bagel and a pat of no-fat cream cheese. *Lunch:* 2 slices turkey breast on whole wheat with 1 cup mayonnaise and four brownies. *Mid-afternoon snack:* 5 bags of chips (not those baked ones) and a vat of real sour cream and onion dip. A large Cherry Coke® with 3 pounds of red Twizzlers®. *Pre-dinner snack:* 1 chocolate cake (only one! You don't want to ruin your appetite). *Dinner:* 6 Big Macs and a Whopper (an equal opportunity party), a strawberry shake and a Frosty from Wendy's. A jumbo order of fries. A Diet Coke®. *Dessert:* A box of Twinkies® with a quart of skim milk.

If you're afraid of having a belly that shakes like a bowl full of jelly every time you bellow "Ho, Ho, Ho", why don't you try . . .

Just Stuff It!

Stamp out Christmas card address stress! Get together with your friends to address Christmas cards. Mail. Then, party.

*I*nvitations

Send a printed invitation with an empty Christmas gift bag large enough to hold a few boxes of Christmas cards. Ask each of your guests to load the bag with their Christmas cards, address book, and stamps.

*A*ttire

Casual writing wear.

Decorations

General Christmas. Set up an area where your guests can spread out and work on their Christmas cards. Have pens and sponges dampened with water (to moisten the stamps and seal the envelopes) available for each guest. After the last envelope is stuffed and stamped, you can all parade over to the closest mailbox and purge yourself of the completed task.

Menu

General Christmas, full bar. Serve wine and tasty morsels (non-oily, non-sticky, non-messy) while you write. Have someone stay at the party site to put out the food while your guests are parading to the post office. Head back home to celebrate!

Favors

Present address books, stamps, pens, and note cards. Your guests will appreciate holiday adorned baskets to hold cards (they can put the cards they just addressed in the basket to carry over to the post office and then use it at home for the cards they'll receive.)

If it isn't in your cards to host this party, why don't you try . . .

The Mad Chatter Tea Party

Here's an opportunity to gather with friends and say whatever is on your mind. Vent. Gossip. Simply chatter. A time to unload and feel better.

Invitations

A tea cup and saucer with the party information written along the rim of the saucer. Daintily toss in a few herbal tea bags, place in a box with some straw, and deliver.

Attire

Flatter Chatter. Wear "tea"-shirts adorned with lace and ribbon, topped off with a ladies-who-do-lunch hat.

Decorations

General Christmas with lace and crocheted doilies and linen tablecloths and napkins. Arrange fresh flowers, such as white tea roses, in crystal vases and bunches of holly in shallow crystal bowls. String white lights. Imagine a Victorian boudoir. You want to feel as if you just waltzed into Victoria's Secret.

Menu

Offer an assortment of nut breads, including date and banana, served with a variety of flavored cream cheeses, softened to spread. Serve cranberry and pumpkin loaves with fresh apple butter and gingerbread and pound cake with fresh whipped cream. Crumpets, scones, jams, jellies, and preserves are delicious treats. Serve tea sandwiches including cucumber and cream cheese, egg salad, tuna salad, chicken salad, and a special sand"witch" (to be eaten while you share your tales of woe about someone that troubles you — a mother-in-law, co-worker, boss, husband, boyfriend, significant other, the neighbor with the barking and dumping dog). Offer a wide assortment of herbal and regular teas served with sugar cubes, honey straws, fresh cream, and lemon wedges.

Favors

Beautifully wrapped *Alice in Wonderland* books. Hand out looking glasses (mirrors) with festive ribbon tied to the handles. Or try teacups filled with mints and wrapped in a lace hanky with the ends gently brought together and tied with a pink satin ribbon.

If too much chatter drives you mad, why don't you try . . .

Chapter ☼ 5

Creative

The next few parties allow your guests to rev up their creative juices and to explore their artistic side. They allow them to get in touch with their true feelings as revealed in the art they create. Okay. Yes, it's getting a little deep. Think more along the lines of a kindergarten arts and crafts class. Purely for fun — no hidden agendas.

Deck Your Halls with Christmas Balls

Your guests will have an opportunity to express their artistic side by designing their own ornaments.

Invitations

Write the party information on a plain Christmas ball ornament using a fine point marker or fabric paint tube. Dot or squiggle lines of glue on the ornament and sprinkle with glitter. When dry, place the ornament in a gift bag filled with straw or shredded paper, adorn with a bow, and hand-deliver. Or, cut circles of heavy paper, write party information on it, decorate, and mail.

Decorations

General Christmas. Place baskets full of colored ball ornaments randomly throughout the party area. If you have a pool, blow up beach balls or large ornament decorations and float them. For fun, guests decorate their own ornaments. Buy plain ornaments and all the adornments. Have miniature bottles of glue for each guest. Arrange all the supplies on a work area where everyone can gather and have a blast.

Menu

Balls! Serve cheese balls, snowballs (cupcakes), meatballs, pizza — any round food (flat or 3-D). This is where your imagination is tested!

Favors

Have personalized Santa caps for all your guests. Use a glitter glue pen to write their names on the white trim. Have a contest for the prettiest ornament, most decorated ball, and other categories. Prizes can be unique ornaments you purchased. Have personalized ornaments made for each of your guests to take home with them.

If the thought of everything in circles makes you dizzy, why don't you try . . .

Just Bare and Trim It

(Or is it "Just grin and bear it?" Either will do). This is a tree trimming party.

Invitations

Take a pine branch and tie with a festive ribbon and a scroll with the party information on it. Or, buy miniature artificial Christmas trees and write the party information on a thin strip of paper and use it to garland the tree. Attach miniature ornaments with a hot glue gun. Put the tree in a brown paper or burlap bag, tie closed with strings of raffia, and stick a fresh pine bough through the knot.

Decorations

General Christmas, without a decorated tree. Your guests will do that with (or for) you. Have all the tree trimmings set up near the tree. Tie ends of everlasting greens with ribbons and bows and place on tables, counter tops, mantles, vanity tops, and other surfaces. Lay serving pieces on top of the boughs which are scattered across green, red, and gold plaid table linens. String miniature lights through the greenery. Finish with a beautiful miniature Christmas tree centerpiece. Play Christmas carols.

Menu

Plan a traditional holiday spread similar to the Light One Up! party.

Favors

For each guest, plant a Christmas tree seedling in a small terra cotta pot with a matching clay saucer. Tie a plaid ribbon and bow around the pot. A personalized ornament is also nice for your guests to take home to adorn their own trees. Have personalized Santa hats for each guest to put on the moment they arrive.

If decorating your tree is your own personal joy, why don't you try . . .

Ye Olde Carefree Card Shoppe

A "personal greeting" meeting. Your guests will have the chance to send holiday greetings without limitation to their loved or "loved" ones by making their own cards. Here's the chance to say what you really want to say that Hallmark can't say.

Invitations

Handmade cards using beautiful paper and glitter in different colors.

Attire

Artsy craftsy.

Decorations

General Christmas. Set up a work table stacked with different color paper, markers, glitter, glue, old Christmas cards (the designs can be cut out and attached to the new ones), scissors, ribbon, fabric, anything you can put on or in a card. Crank up the carols and get creative!

Menu

Your guests will be in the mood to make their anything-goes cards as soon as they relax a bit. Your job, should you choose to accept it, is to feed 'em good food and drinks! Provide carefree and creative foods in step with the cards your guests will make.

Favors

Have prizes for card categories — most festive, nastiest, most clever, best verse, most poetic, and so on. Gift certificates from

Hallmark or another card store, boxes of note cards, a beautiful pen or a box of Christmas thank-you notes are lovely gifts.

If you've discovered an underground card shop that you've already turned your friends on to, why don't you try . . .

Gingerbread People Party

Your guests will have a great time decorating politically correct gingerbread people!

Invitations

Gingerbread people with the party information iced on it or just attached. Use a paper cutout or the real thing. (Caution! If you send real cookies (edible) your guests might eat them and have no record where they're supposed to be and when.) Or, glue the party information to the back of a box of gingerbread mix. Ribbon, bow, and deliver.

Attire

Gingerbread garb (unisex).

Decorations

General Christmas decorations will do. The focal point will be the cookie decorating work space. Fill bowls with sprinkles, sugar crystals, nonpareils, candies, raisins, chocolate chips, etc. Have tubes of fine-line icing in different colors and tubes of thick white frosting for each guest. You'll need plain, unadorned gingerbread people cookies for your guests to decorate. Make sure you have lots of gingerbread people on hand - bake 'em or buy 'em — just get 'em. More is better. Place brown paper bag gingerbread people in all sizes around the party area. They're a snap to make. Trace the outline of a gingerbread person on a sheet of brown packaging paper (grocery bags can be used for medium size gingerbread people). Place another sheet of paper under the one with the design and cut out (you'll end up with two the same size). Draw a face on one of the cut-outs, gluing on buttons for the eyes, and so forth, if you'd like. Sew the two pieces together along the edges, using a heavy needle and some red yarn. Don't close the head. Stuff cotton through the opening in the head to fill the "cookie's" body. When plump enough, sew shut.

Menu

General Christmas quickie food and beverage ideas. Use ginger wherever possible. It's an excellent flavor for chicken and fish dishes. Serve iced gingerbread squares and gingersnaps.

Favors

Have prizes for various categories of gingerbread people — ugliest, prettiest, scariest, most festive, most boring, most delicious. Buy plastic bags imprinted with a holiday message from a party supply store — these are to be used to transport the decorated goodies home. Give personalized aprons and chef hats to all your guests (use a tube of fabric paint or a permanent marker) or bakery decorated gingerbread people, personalized with the names of your guests.

If your guests aren't into decorating people with foodstuffs no matter how politically correct, why don't you try . . .

Chapter 6

It Just Doesn't Matter

Before you read any further, stand up and put your hands on your hips. Now, in your most authoritative voice repeat these words out loud three times: "Who cares! I have a right to have fun and I'm gonna have it!" You are now ready to read on and pick one (or all three) of the parties in this chapter to act on your words —to prove you mean what you say and say what you mean. Get wild and crazy — let your hair down (and if you have none, wear an outrageous wig). Remember . . . all that matters is that you're living your life the way you want to. And once you do, you'll be blessed with holiday fun days every day starting today.

(Lamp) Shades of the Season

This party is a take on the old joke about having so much "fun" at a party that the guests ended up wearing lamp shades before the party was over. Supposedly, the people who ended up with lamp shades on their heads had way too much to drink and made a fool of themselves. That's not the goal of this party, yet it's close. The idea isn't to get so loaded that you're rendered clueless. The purpose of this party is to not really give a darn what other people think of you, so you can drop all your pretenses if you have any, lighten up, and make a fool out of yourself just because you can. It's a "who-cares-I'm-having-fun" party. Go ahead, wear a lamp shade. See if I care!

Invitations

If you can find some tiny white shades, grab them (pay for them first). Or, make your own by rolling white poster board using a lamp-shade in your house as a guide. Write the party information on the shade and festively decorate with red, white, and gold glitter and other items you find that symbolize holiday good times.

Attire

Could care-less couture. Wear clothes that don't match because it just doesn't matter. You know — one of those "got-dressed-in-the-dark" get-ups . . . and lamp shades (the little invitation or a big one from home).

Decorations

General Christmas with special attention to the lamps in the party area. Drape the shades with clothes, scraps of fabric, dirty socks (not really, but hey, it's your party — you may want to). You're trying to show that you didn't have to do a thing for this party because the theme is not to care what others think. In other words, it's okay to leave the sink full of that morning's breakfast dishes (but I'd strongly suggest that you make sure last year's dishes are out of there!)

Menu

Anything you'd like to serve. WHO CARES! So long as it's edible and drinkable, it'll work.

Favors

Have prizes on hand for the best "I don't care!" lampshade and most mismatched attire. For example, hand out gift certificates from a lamp and lighting store. Everyone takes a decorated box of bulbs home. Have votive candles and matchbooks on hand for those who should give up on lamp shades for good.

If all your clothes match (or at least you think they do) and you have recessed lighting in your home (nary a lampshade in sight), why don't you try . . .

Disco Here, Disco There — Dancin' Elves Everywhere!

A tribute to the 70's. Dance Fever with a Peppermint Twist.

Invitations

Unless John Travolta has agreed to handwrite the invitations for you, printed ones will do. Or glue the party information on to some old 8-track tapes. Stuff the envelopes with silver tinsel (reminiscent of the mirror balls over the dance floor). Pop in some "Merry Christmas" confetti. Plan this one for a Saturday night to get the fever going!!

Attire

Dashing through the snow disco duds. Men can wear shirts unbuttoned to their navels with ropes of gold chains circling their necks and a white three piece suit. Women can wear anything in polyester with platform shoes and Farrah Fawcett hair. Add some elf ears and you'll be sending the world a strong message that you've got the fever and you're ready to boogie on down with your bad self.

Decorations

General Christmas with tacky disco stuff including a strobe light and a mirrored dance ball. Make sure you have room for a dance floor. That's what this is all about — shaking booty and strutting your stuff. Hire a disc jockey to pump out those seventies sounds! Definitely get the *Saturday Night Fever* soundtrack and video. Play both throughout the night. Hire a dance instructor to teach you and your guests how to really get down, get down and shake your groove thing.

Menu

You're supposed to "feed a cold and starve a fever". You could get out of serving your guests anything under this theory, but it is the holiday season after all and what would a party be without food? General Christmas is all you need.

Favors

Send your guests home with a soundtrack or video of THE movie and other "music" from the era for disco dance wizards and lounge lizards. Other favor ideas include gold chains (gold-plated is good enough) wrapped around a candy cane, a thermometer to measure the dance fever, and bottles of aspirin to bring the fever down.

If the thought of gold chains tangled in masses of chest hair bring on an automatic gag reflex, why don't you try . . .

Flamingo Holiday Fest

Flamingoes are really cool birds. They're always feeling in the pink, never blue. They just hang out and mind their own business. They love to be in crowds. Have you ever seen only one flamingo standing alone in a National Geographic documentary? Never. In fact, there are usually hundreds if not thousands of them packed together. They are very social birds. Which, in my opinion means big-time party birds. Why not have a party in honor of them?

Invitations

Flamingo ornaments with the party information attached, packed in a straw-filled box with some flamingo and Christmas confetti. Or, cut out flamingo shapes from bright pink paper. Cut out a wing from a separate piece of paper to place on the cut-out. Glue the top part only. You want to be able to lift the wing to find the party information. Color in the eyes, beak, and legs. Print the party information under the wing. Place in an envelope. Add some pink feathers and Christmas confetti.

Attire

Pink panache.

Decorations

Place pink flamingoes in your yard. It matters not whether your lawn is green or white. Wrap the flamingoes with white lights, Santa hats, and mufflers. Plastic lawn flamingos can be found in the garden section of stores like K-Mart. If you can't find any plastic ones, cut silhouettes from heavy paper, paint, nail to a wood stake, and place in the ground. Then bring the pink indoors. Decorate in General Christmas with pink as the main color. Tie pink bows and ribbons wherever you can. Glue flamingoes to grapevine wreaths and hang. Exchange your regular light bulbs for pink ones in your lamps.

Menu

Serve pink salmon and shrimp boats. Pour pink champagne. (*See* Beach Blanket Gift Wrap party and Island Christmas: Yo Man! party for other tropical ideas.)

Favors

Everyone takes home a personalized flamingo ornament. A bottle of pink champagne with a silk poinsettia tied to the neck of the bottle is also a special memento.

If you aren't exactly (or any other way) tickled pink over this one, why don't you try . . .

Chapter ☀ 7

Traditional &

Special

In this chapter you'll find four warm and fuzzy feeling holiday parties — traditional gatherings and special get-togethers with some extra zing, zip, spice, and splash. Whatever you're celebrating — Christmas or just because it's December — you'll find a lively take on the celebration that is dear to us. No doubt Christmas is a very serious celebration, representing significant events behind our beliefs. However, this serious holiday deserves a fun-day twist, since no matter what our beliefs are, we all need and desire love, laughter, creativity, and originality. The ideas you'll find in this chapter have these needs and desires in mind and aren't intended to diminish the importance of this event, but to expand on it to capture the joy and spirit for living each of us has in our heart. Enjoy!

Light One Up!

An enlightened traditional gathering.

Invitations

Place a votive candle and matchbox with the party information imprinted on it in a gift bag or box (imprinted matchboxes can be ordered from shops that offer personalized invitations and stationery). You could also wrap a taper candle with a sheet of paper with the party information on it, secure with a ribbon, and place in a mailing tube.

Decorations

Easy! Lighting is the focus of the party and is achieved by natural and artificial sources. Line your driveway, walkway, entry way — every which way — with luminaries. (*See* Chapter One for how-to's.) Put candles everywhere for that holiday glow! Float candles (there are candles made specially to do this) in bowls of water, your bathtub, and, if you have one, a swimming pool. For a soft glow from your artificial bulbs, drape sheets of organza, gauze, and/or tulle over your lamp shades.

Menu

Serve a candlelight buffet (candelabra) with traditional food — turkey, stuffing, gravy, flaky rolls, whipped potatoes, candied yams, cranberry sauce, and pumpkin pie and cinnamon ice cream.

Favors

Present your guests with key chain flashlights, scented candles, and imprinted matchbooks.

If you don't think this party is a bright idea, why don't you try . . .

A Flower Powered Party

Legend has it in Mexico that a young boy, who couldn't afford to bring a gift to the crèche, knelt to offer a prayer instead. A poinsettia grew where the boy's knee touched the ground. Wow! What power. This party is held in honor of this power flower. Think of what power beautiful flowers have over you. How do you feel when a beautiful floral arrangement is delivered to you, especially on a rotten day? That's what this party will do for your spirits.

Invitations

A poinsettia with the party information attached to a florist's stick and planted in the flower's soil, and hand-delivered. You can use any size plant, real or artificial. One flower placed in a box filled with shredded tissue or metallic paper in white, gold, or green with the party information makes a dramatic statement.

Attire

Poinsettia pleasant. Put flowers on hats, ties, lapels, just about anywhere. Just have them somewhere. If you used a single silk flower as part of your invitation, ask your guests to wear it to the party (creatively).

Decorations

Your General Christmas infused with a flood of poinsettias. There are many poinsettia patterned tablecloths, napkins, and serving dishes available during the season. Red solids can be used with touches of flowers here and there. You could place a red tablecloth on your serving table and scatter poinsettias, real or artificial, across it, cutting the stem close to the base of the flower so it will lay flat. If you use real flowers, you'll notice a milky white, sticky sap that comes from the stem. To stop the flow, strike a match and sear the cut end with the flame. Add gold tinsel and white or red lights between the serving pieces to complete the spread.

Menu

General Christmas. Concoct a "Poinsettia Power Punch". Skim through holiday cookbooks for a red punch recipe and rename it to suit your party. Make an ice ring using artificial plastic poinsettias. Visit your bakery. There are lovely cakes and candies this time of the year decorated with or made to look like poinsettias without you having to go through the hassle.

Favors

Have prizes for the most creative placement of the poinsettia. Everyone takes home one of the poinsettias that you used to decorate the party area. Any remaining plants can be brought to a nursing home.

If just the name of this party evokes strong flashbacks to those other "flower power" days and you're a tad bit uncomfortable, why don't you try . . .

Scrooge's Progressive-Regressive Dinner Party

Meet the past, present, and yet to come. Get a group of your friends to take on different parts of the evening. One house will host the hors d'oeuvres and cocktails in celebration of the past, another will host the appetizer and salad with another hosting the entree, both in celebration of the present. The final stop is the yet-to-come dessert. You'll note that Scrooge, being a scrooge doesn't host anything! It's all up to you and your friends.

Invitations

Invite as many people as the four hosts can accommodate. Everyone gets the party information attached to a copy of Charles Dickens' *A Christmas Carol*. Include the progressive dinner destinations and menus.

Attire

Past, present, or future. Whatever is suitable for the kind of evening you had in mind. Holiday casual to cocktail to black tie. Make sure the hosts dress according to their roles (past, present, or future).

Decorations

General Christmas is enough, however, each site should carry out the theme of past, present, and yet-to-be. This can be achieved using the theme of each Christmas Carol ghost (skim through the book and notice how each ghost presents itself) or in some other creative way (perhaps bring the fortune-tellers back from Prediction: You Will Attend an Awesome Party?).

Menu

Each host will coordinate what they'd like to serve. So long as the food is compatible, anything is appropriate.

Favors

Each host site should have a remembrance for each guest. For example, the "past" household could pass out gift wrapped past-life regression cassettes or a copy of a book on the subject such as *Many Lives, Many Masters* by Dr. Brian Weiss. The "present" hosts have it easy — they just need to wrap up a present. As for the yet-to-come hosts, a pack of Tarot cards would be in the spirit of things.

If you believe Bah Humbug is a perfectly acceptable holiday greeting, yet you still want to have a party (why?), why don't you try . . .

We ♡ Christmas

Invitations

A red paper or wood heart with a sprig of mistletoe packed in a satin drawstring pouch with the party information included. (Trivia time-out: Did you know that Norse legend has it that mistletoe not only brings you a kiss, but luck and fertility, too? You'll be sending your friends wishes for a happy and bountiful new year). You can also deliver a heart shaped helium balloon with a mistletoe "weight" (tied to the end of the string to anchor the balloon). A heart in a clear vellum envelope with the party information written or printed in gold ink with red metallic heart and "Merry Christmas" or "Happy Holidays" confetti sprinkled inside the envelope.

Attire
Holiday heart wear: Red, red, and . . . more red. A big heart.

Decorations
General Christmas with splashes of love. Hang red hearts of all different materials — wood, paper, metal, fabric, and glass in a variety of sizes on your tree. Add strands of red lights. Play Christmas love ballads. Place lots of angels around the party area. Hang mistletoe in every doorway.

Menu
Serve love foods. Here are some to consider: Lobster, crab, clams, rare steak, vanilla, ginger, rosemary, oysters, hearts of palm, tomatoes, and, of course, chocolate. For other ideas read *The Foods of Love* by Max de Roche.

Favors
Your guests will love a heart paperweight, a tender book on Christmas love, forgiveness, and peace, or a sprig of mistletoe presented in a beautiful miniature basket.

If this is heart-ly your kind of party, why don't you try . . .

Chapter ☀ 8

The Movies

I'm not much of a television person. Never have been, even as a child. However, when the holiday specials are aired, I wrestle the remote from my husband and settle into a comfortable chair, throw a quilt over my lap, sip hot chocolate, and allow myself to escape from every day life into the magic the movies create. Having lived in Florida most of my life, my dreams of a white Christmas come true only if I transport myself via plane to some northern destination or stay put in front of the tube, with my imagination piloting me to snow covered territory where the real Santa visits the most incredibly decorated 5th Avenue shops. I took a few of my favorites and built a party around them. Transport you and your guests to a magical holiday spot without leaving the comfort of your home.

It's a Wonderful Life!

This party was inspired by the movie of the same name. *It's a Wonderful Life* is all about helping a friend. Our version requires you to do the same by helping someone. The way you do this is by bringing someone to the party. Anyone! Think of all the new friendships that can be cultivated.

Invitations

How about attaching the party information to the back of the soundtrack (CD or cassette) of the hit television series "Friends"? If you'd rather save the soundtrack to use as party favors, a printed "bring a friend" invite is all you need. The important thing, whatever form you use, is to make it clear that the person you invited is to bring someone with them (sort of like an admission ticket).

Attire

Friendly fashion (whatever you think that means). Comfortable? Casual? Caring?

Decorations

General Christmas with the "Friends" soundtrack playing in the background. You could also put taped television shows of "Friends" on your VCR. (Make sure you have the holiday special in your collection).

Menu

This is another one of those whatever you want to serve parties. In keeping with the theme, you might want to rename your favorite food or drink. For example, Friendly Froth (the big keg of beer sitting in the corner waiting to be tapped) or Friendliest Frittata (a Mexican egg dish). The key is to celebrate old friends, new friends, friends to be.

Favors

"Friends" soundtracks, T-shirts, and other products are great mementos, as are pocket-size books on friendship or the paperback version of *How to Win Friends and Influence People* by Dale Carnegie. Friendship rings (the kind you get from a bubble gum machine) are sweet gifts.

If you have enough friends or prefer to have none, why don't you try . . .

Miracle on 34th Street

This party was also inspired by the movie of the same name. Your guests will take a trip to a department store or mall, preferably Macy's, to sit on Santa's lap and tell him all their wants and desires.

Invitations

The party information has to come direct from the North Pole and it must be from the real Santa Claus. Print this message or some variation on your invitation: "Heard of the Miracle on 34th Street? Well, there's a miracle on (put your address here). Be there (or be nowhere)." How you do it isn't as important as who does it. Once again, it must be the real thing. In case you're in doubt about the Santa you found roaming the street, tug his beard twice (not too hard) and double-check the sparkle in his eye before you invite him to address your invitations. After the big guy has finished all the addresses on his list and checked them twice, you can stuff them into envelopes, seal, stamp, and mail.

Attire

Sit-on-Santa's-lap appropriate.

Decorations

General Christmas, general mall, or general department store. Instead of taking a field trip to the mall, you could invite Santa to come to your party. Set your place up like a department store. With the help of lots of shopping bags, you can easily recreate the scene without leaving home. The only must-do is that the REAL Santa has to be there. Invite the Santa that addressed your invitations since he has already been tested (a very important social thing these days).

Menu

Create a food court at the mall spread. Serve stuffed potatoes, Chinese food, Sbarro's pizza slices, and orange juliuses. Barnies® coffee and cookies will be most welcome. Don't forget a "house special" drink from the mall's restaurant bar where the guy that may be in your life usually hangs out while you shop (in my case, Ruby Tuesday — they have a special drink that has malted milk balls in it — add a few to Reindeer Milk for something close).

Favors

Give everyone a gift certificate to a popular store. Some of the larger stores will give you special fragrance samples from their cosmetic counters and discount coupons for general store use. Check with the store you do business with well in advance to give them time to help you out. If your guests have a sense of humor, you can always hand out lumps of coal.

If it would be a miracle if you are able to you pull this one off, why don't you try . . .

Home Alone (But Not for Long)

Invite your friends over to watch the movies *Home Alone I* and *Home Alone II* while they plan the trip of their dreams. This party allows you to escape the hustle and bustle of the season by planning your dream trip outta here, even if it's only in your mind (to keep you from going out of your mind).

Invitations

Staple the party information to a small world atlas or map. Ask your guests to start thinking of their dream trip and to be ready to travel! You could also put a little globe in a gift bag, fill with shredded tissue, add the party information, and deliver.

Attire

Travel-well, wrinkle-free. Dress the way the natives do where you'd love to visit with a holiday twist. For example, if you've always dreamed of a Caribbean cruise, put on a tropical shirt, white shorts, black socks, and sandals. Or, wear a grass skirt, coconut shell bra, and a flower in your hair. Or, if you've always wanted to go to France, wear a beret and carry a baguette adorned with a Christmas plaid ribbon. Or, perhaps, Germany is your dream destination. Snap some suspenders onto your pants, carry a stein, and sling a string of Bratwurst over your shoulder.

Decorations

General Christmas with international touches. Go to a travel agency and pick up brochures from places all over the world. Put travel posters on your walls (simply tape to existing wall hangings). Put a globe on your serving table surrounded by greenery and lights. Show the *Home Alone* movies and serve popcorn.

Menu

An international hors d'oeuvres buffet is the way to go. Chinese, Mexican, French, Germany, American — flip through cookbooks and find simple recipes from other countries. Or, simply walk through the frozen food aisle of your grocery store and pick up some egg rolls, burritos, French fries, and sausages, and other pop in the oven delights. Have shakers full of popcorn toppings such as grated parmesan, cheddar and other cheeses, butter, garlic salt, chili powder, and cinnamon sugar for show time.

Favors

Everyone leaves with a travel log and a pen or pencil imprinted with the party information on it. A roll of film is also a good idea.

If running errands all day long is enough traveling for you and if your idea of a dream trip is to be "Home Alone," why don't you try . . .

Chapter 9

International

Welcome to the international party section. I've taken some real traditions and mixed them with some stereotypes. As with every party in this book, the underlying goal is to fill your guests hearts with love and laughter. For no matter what nationality we are — what and how we celebrate — love and laughter are universal desires. We only go around once, and this round the world series of parties is one way to make the most of it. Enjoy your holiday visits to France, Germany, Italy, Mexico, Ireland, and a one-stop joyous jaunt around the world. Love and laughter to all!

Party with an Attitude: A French Fête

Joyeux Noël! (Merry Christmas!)

Invitations

A loaf of French bread tied with red and green ribbon with the party information attached to it. Or, staple the party information to a map of France.

Attire

French chic with an attitude. Wear a beret with a pair of jeans and a white T-shirt or a Chanel™ suit from Karl Lagerfeld's celebrated holiday collection. In other words, anything. Just make sure to cop an attitude by the time the party begins.

Decorations

Try to create a sidewalk cafe atmosphere. Rent small bistro tables for your guests to sit at while watching the other guests stroll by. Place potted flowers all over. Put white twinkling lights on all the trees and plants. Play some carols from France, such as "O Holy Night", "Angels We Have Heard on High", "He Is Born ("Il Est Ne")", and "Whence, O Shepherd Maiden?" Hang France travel posters on existing wall hangings. Frame the posters with garland and red, white, and blue ornaments. A three dimensional Eiffel Tower (available at The Pottery Barn) decorated with lights and ornaments can be used as a center-piece for your serving table.

Menu

Serve lots of wine, bread, wine, cheese, wine, fruit, and wine. Croissants are a must. Do as the French do and serve oysters as an appetizer with a traditional Christmas holiday bird — either a goose or a turkey. For the grand finale, wheel out a traditional holiday dessert, Bûche de Noël (a chocolate-frosted, cream-filled cake roll). If you've cooked your goose in the non-edible way, serve French fries and French onion soup. Bon Appetit!

Favors

You know how Santa leaves gifts in our stockings? Well, in France, gifts are left in shoes (no wonder I have an obsession with France and shoes). How much loot your guests will walk away with seems to depend on the size of one's feet. Small feet will be discriminated against (I see another protected class surfacing). (Guest tip: Bring along a pair of Aunt Sabina's size eleven boats and swap them for your size seven's when no one is looking). Ask your guests to remove their shoes as they arrive, then fill them with little treats such as miniature rounds of brie, a wine stopper, samples of French perfume, and coupons for McDonald's French fries.

If you've been to France and the natives treated you so badly that all you want to do is fry the French, why don't you try . . .

German Shepherds

Fröhliche Weinachten! (Merry Christmas!) No, not the dogs, the shepherds. Oktoberfest in December.

Invitations

A bottle of Beck's® or St. Pauli Girl® with the party information attached and placed in a brown paper bag. Twist the top of the paper bag around the neck of the bottle. Or, staple the party information to a map of Germany.

Attire

Shepherd social. Put on some suspenders, shorts, and knee-hi socks all covered by a long flowing robe.

Decorations

General Christmas is fine, however, try to Germanize the party area. Pick up some travel brochures from a travel agent and try to duplicate what you see. Play German carols such as the "The Christmas Nightingale", "Stille Nacht", and "Tannen Baum". Do beer barrel polkas or the chicken dance.

Menu

Serve bratwursts and knockwursts with an assortment of mustards, pickles, sauerkraut, and beer by the gallon. Offer Lebkuchen and Pfeffernüsse for dessert.

Favors

Christkind Angel brings the gifts in Germany. So, play angel and give your guests a gift bag filled with straw, mustard, and a sausage or two.

If you're still recovering from Oktoberfest (even though it's December), why don't you try . . .

Very Merry Mobsters

Buon Natale! (Merry Christmas!) This is a great party if your friends are all partied out and must be coerced to attend yet another one. You will have fun, or else . . .

Invitations

Attach the party information to a shaker container of parmesan cheese or a box of pasta. Pack in a small unmarked bag. Toss in some laundered shredded tissue in holiday colors. Seal with duct tape, and do as a special delivery.

Attire

Gala gangster. Pinstriped anything will be right on target. Slick back your hair and fill your cheeks with cotton balls (Guest tip: Take the cotton out of your mouth before you hit the pasta bar!) Wear cement shoes. All weapons must be concealed and capable of shooting a stream of water no farther than 15 feet.

Decorations

Red, white, and green are the colors of Italy which so happen to be the colors of Christmas. Turn the party area into an Italian kitchen. Red and white checked napkins and tablecloths. Stack unopened boxes of different kinds of pasta on the serving table. Add some cans of tomatoes and garlic heads. Bottles of olive oil and a large pot of homemade sauce simmering on the stove. Stick candles in empty bottles of Chianti (the bottle in the basket). Play Italian carols, including the traditional favorite "Carol of the Bagpipes". Invite some bagpipers to play for you and your guests. (Be wary if one of the musicians shows up with a violin case). Frank Sinatra Christmas carols. Have The Godfather play Santa: "You **will** have a Merry Christmas. Ho Ho Ho! You **will** love what I bring you. Ho Ho Ho!"

Menu

Serve all kinds of pasta with all kinds of sauces. Place bowls of grated parmesan cheese around the table. Have baskets full of garlic rolls and plain Italian bread served with olive oil and roasted garlic heads. Bruscetta is a popular appetizer and is surprisingly easy to make. Here's a recipe for the tastiest bruscetta in this country compliments of my good friend, Chef Giacomo.

Giacomo's Tomato & Basil Bruscetta
(serves 4-6)

1 loaf sour dough or whole wheat bread (no white bread - it's too soft)

1 cup extra virgin olive oil

4 ripe tomatoes, chopped

fresh oregano, chopped

1 cup fine minced garlic

1 cup finely chopped red onion

1 cup basil julienne

1 cup balsamic vinegar

$\frac{1}{4}$ pound romano cheese, grated

1 cup parsley chopped

$\frac{1}{2}$ teaspoon seasoning

salt & white pepper

Slice bread (medium cut). Spread with olive oil and bake at 350° F for 4 to 5 minutes or until golden brown. Set aside. Combine all the ingredients in a bowl except the romano cheese and a little parsley and basil to garnish. Add salt and pepper to taste. Spoon out some of the mixture and put on top of bread. Place on a serving plate and sprinkle with romano cheese, basil, and parsley.

(Note: This recipe is a family secret so, please, don't share it with anyone).

Other Italian holiday traditions include serving capitone (eel), panettone (bread filled with fruits), and capon. Dessert can be trays of assorted Italian cookies and cannolis with coffees and liqueurs. Consider serving fish chunks in marinara sauce (loan shark bites) or an icebox cake (cement block cake).

Favors

La Befana brings the gifts in Italy. La Befana was an old woman who was too busy sweeping when asked to join the Wise Men on their journey to bear gifts for baby Jesus. She regretted not going, so took off on her own, soaring on the broomstick she was just using, to look for the Christ Child, leaving gifts for all children just in case one was the Child she was looking for. Be La Befana and give each of your guests a little gift such as a pocket guide on how to speak Italian. "The Godfather" book or video, water pistols with red ribbons tied to the trigger, or Pavarotti or Frank Sinatra CD's or cassettes, jars of homemade spaghetti sauce, a can or bottle of olive oil, and a box of pasta placed in a holiday gift bag are great take-home treats.

If you're in the witness protection program and are prone to flashbacks of a previous life, why don't you try . . .

Fiesta, Then Siesta

Feliz Navidad! (Merry Christmas!) Everything moves at a more relaxed pace in Mexico than in other parts of the world. It's an enviable pace, especially during the holidays. This party, in keeping in step with the movement (a snail triathlon), is the opposite of "eat and run" and "dine and dash". This is a nosh and nap holiday party. Do the fiesta then take a siesta! Muy bien!

Invitations

Attach the party information to a sombrero and deliver. Or, glue the information to the back of a taco kit box or to a jar of salsa (send with a bag of chips).

Attire

All that's required is a sombrero. (If you don't send one with the invitation, let your guests know that there will be one with their name on it at the fiesta.)

Decorations

Mexico's colors are also red, white, and green. Hang streamers and float balloons with these colors. Hang piñatas anywhere you can (they don't have to be filled). Create a fiesta atmosphere using lots of bright colors. Cover the serving table with yellow, pink, green, and red clothes. Inexpensive, colorful tablecloths, napkins, paper plates, cups, and matching utensils can be bought at any party outlet. Make a cactus Christmas tree centerpiece. Put a live or artificial cactus in a terra cotta pot filled with stones to balance the plant. Adorn with lights and brightly painted papier mâché ornaments.

Menu

Start off with some snacks. Serve salsa, guacamole, and black bean dip and chips. To make a festive dip, layer refried beans, sour cream, diced tomatoes, black olives (sliced and drained), and shredded cheddar and jack cheese. Serve with tortilla and corn chips. Your guests will load their own tacos, roll their own burritos, and fill their own fajitas. A real workout! (Whew! Bring me a margarita). Set up an assembly line serving table. Include baskets full of taco shells and warm tortillas, bowls of shredded lettuce, chopped tomatoes, diced onions, shredded cheese, sliced jalapeno peppers, and taco sauce. Make sure you have ground beef or sirloin or ground turkey prepared according to the directions on the back of the taco seasoning packet and some sizzling strips of beef and chicken for the fajitas. Offer bean dip to spread and salsa to pour on the burritos. Have a margarita bar set up with tequila and various margarita mixes — they come in many flavors. You can rent margarita glasses and pitchers if you don't have enough. Don't forget the salt for the glass rims. Wedge some limes, too. Have some shot glasses around for the diehards, for all those José Cuervos® amigos in the crowd. Worms are optional (have a jar of Gummi Worms® for palatable fun). And don't forget to pick up some Sangria. Add sliced oranges to a store-bought bottle. Offer cinnamon tortilla strips for dessert with fried ice cream — roll scoops of ice-cream in Grapenut cereal, drizzle chocolate sauce on top, and freeze.

Favors

In Mexico, the Three Wise Men bring the gifts. For your party, be the wise guy and make sure your guests leave home with something such as a personalized sombrero, a bag of Doritos, and a jar of home-made salsa.

If you think the Frito Bandito is muy finito, why don't you try . . .

Wearin' of the Green In December

Every day is St. Patty's day through Irish eyes. Let this party be a prelude to the official March 17th holiday. A practice session or simply a warm-up if you will. If anything, it's just another excuse to party.

Invitations

A red shamrock with the party information on it, placed in an envelope with some green shamrock confetti.

Attire

Leprechaun looking good.

Decorations

Think bagpipes and blarney stones. Hang shamrocks from the Christmas tree. Arrange for an Irish Santa with an intoxicating personality to amuse your guests. Have him wear some Notre Dame skivvies under his Santa suit.

Menu

Serve Irish stew and chunks of soda bread. Pour lots of beer and whiskey. On that note, here's a recipe for Irish Punch: 6 ounces Irish Whiskey, 2 tablespoons honey, lemon slices, ¼ cup boiled water. Rinse two heavy mugs with hot water. Put one tablespoon of honey in the bottom of each and add half of the water to dissolve the honey. Heat whiskey in a pan (don't boil) and add to mugs. Top each with a lemon slice. And have another! Those Irish are always one step ahead. They already know how to drink green beer. They just have to get used to some red beer to release the full Christmas spirit (if this is going to be a problem, Killian's Red® is acceptable).

Favors

A loaf of Irish soda bread tied with a Scottish plaid ribbon will make those Irish eyes smile.

If you're still feelin' a wee bit green from last March 17th, why don't you try (if you can't stop partying for a while) . . .

Joy To the World

Let's end this chapter with a universal party celebrating all countries.

Invitations

Small globe balls (I've seen them at toy stores) with the party information written directly on the sphere. Staple the party information to world maps, or attach them to "Joy to the World" sheet music.

Attire

Joyful worldly wraps. Wear the colors and style of your ancestors.

Decorations

General Christmas with flags from the world. Place a few caged doves around the party area (you can buy a pair or two from a pet shop and some party planners can rent them). Scatter olive branches. Turn on a "Joy to the World" soundtrack that plays, and plays and plays . . . until promises of world peace are exchanged for a promise to not play "that song" again. Visit a travel agent and pick up some travel brochures from around the world. Most agents will gladly give you as many brochures as you'd like, especially if they think you're planning a lap around the planet.

Menu

The international buffet suggested in Home Alone (But Not for Long) party would be perfect. Serve Almond Joy® bars, Dove® ice cream bars, Dove® chocolate bars, and Dove Promises® (chocolate squares wrapped in foil that, when opened, reveal a sweet written message) in milk and dark chocolate are to be devoured in the name of peace. (Ponder the effect of this. If all people of this world committed to chocolate in times of strife, world peace could be a reality. Think of the role the Swiss government could play!)

Favors

Hand your guests doggie bags full of Dove and Almond Joy bars. Present travel atlases, airline ticket holders, and other travel novelties, such as luggage locks and luggage tags.

If having joy in your world doesn't include having this party, why don't you try . . .

Chapter ☼ 10 ☼

Noise

Make it loud and clear that you're here to spread holiday cheer! And that's exactly what you'll do with these parties. Your intentions to party hardy will definitely be heard as you bid your guests (and everyone else within earshot) a joyous holiday with a microphone in one hand and a bunch of bells in the other. Within the pages of this chapter, you'll find four ways to sing and ring your greetings! Clear your throat, get a little jingle going, and have a blast!

Anything But a Silent Night

This party was inspired in honor of my good friend Burt who never met a microphone he didn't love (or a party for that matter!) The star of this party is the Karaoke machine. Many of the new stereo systems and entertainment centers have Karaoke jacks built in. If yours does, all you'll need is a microphone. If not, you can rent or borrow a machine.

Invitations

Staple the party information to a Christmas carol book or the sheet music for "Silent Night". Roll the book and place in a mailing tube. Sprinkle some musical note confetti in the tube and add some shredded tissue in red or green or both before sealing.

Attire

Cool stage clothes.

Decorations

General Christmas is all you need. The focal point will be on the Karaoke machine. Prominently place it near "the stage". I can hear it now. "Oh, yeah, sure. A stage in my house." You'd be surprised how much room you can create when you park the kids toys in the garage, haul all those newspapers, magazines, and catalogs that you'll get to "when you have time" to the recycler, and do this week's (and last week's and the week's before) laundry and put it away before your guests arrive. (Hey, that just gave me an idea — a laundry party — your guests bring their red, green, and white clothes over to be washed, dried, and folded . . . never mind . . .) or it can be a real big deal where you rent a stage and create your own sets (a Christmas tree, plastic Santas and reindeers, you get the picture). And speaking of pictures, a video camera is a must. The money you raise from your guests "how-much-will-it-take-for you-to-destroy-the-tape" loot can be donated to charity. Move over Frank Sinatra and Madonna. You might want to consider spreading the holiday cheer by taking your act on the road, for example, to a nursing home (all you may be required to do is provide earplugs to those who don't have hearing aids that can be turned down or off). In addition to the Karaoke machine and your vocal cords, bring Hershey Kisses® and Hershey Hugs® for your audience.

Menu
The General Christmas spread will do, however, you might have to double your bar stock!

Favors
Have a contest for best voice, worst voice, highest voice, best overall act (singers dance too, you know). Some suggested prizes include a Mr. Microphone (a child's toy), a personal use Karaoke machine (they aren't that expensive), and gift certificates for voice lessons. Everyone goes home with earplugs!

If you'd give your firstborn for just one silent night (a real quiet one), why don't you try . . .

Hark the Herald Angels Sing . . . and So Do You!

Burt Act II.

Invitations
Angels in a bag inviting your guests to join them in singing sounds of joy. There are many angel invitations that you can use. You could even use blank note cards and write the party information inside of it.

Ornaments are a good idea, too. Sheet music for "Hark the Herald Angels Sing" with the party information stapled to it.

Attire

Choir clothes (Any altar boys out there?) Halos and wings encouraged.

Decorations

Set up a stage just like in Anything But a Silent Night party yet make this one heavenly. Add a light blue sky backdrop and some fluffy clouds. Gold and white are your colors for this one. Surround your party area with angels. For an extravagant touch, rent one of those dry ice machines that are used on nightclub dance floors to provide a misty atmosphere.

Menu

Serve angel hair pasta with a variety of sauces (cream, marinara, primavera). Place baskets full of chunks of Italian bread served with roasted garlic heads, olive, and real butter. Delight your guests with other foods of the Gods. For dessert, offer angel food cake served with a variety of toppings — fresh whipped cream, raspberry sauce, chocolate sauce, sliced strawberries and other fruit, powdered sugar. Brew some coffee and serve with assorted liqueurs. (*See* The Cake.)

Favors

There are so many angel products on the market today that you won't have any problems finding terrific favors. Pick up some note cards or notepads. Hand out "You're an Angel" certificates. Have a prize on hand for the most angelic voice such as a cute cherub figurine. Offer each of your guests a guardian angel pin.

If your halo is tarnished and your wings have been clipped, why don't you try . . .

A Jingle Bell Bash

Invitations

Find printed bell-shaped invitations, place in clear vellum envelopes, and add a few jingle bells. Seal with bell-shaped stickers (if you can't find them any Christmas symbol will do). Your guests will open the invite, the bells will fall out with a jingle, prompting your guest to give you a jingle to R.S.V.P.

Attire

Jingle, jangle casual. Wear a bell somewhere. Pull on a pair of bell bottom jeans.

Decorations

General Christmas with an emphasis on bells (now that's a surprise!). Hang bells on every doorknob your guests could turn. All you need to do is cut Christmas ribbon (¼-inch width) in two foot lengths. Sew a bell to each end. Gather about five of these belled ribbons and hang over a door knob — tie all the strands together and knot under the knob to secure.

Menu

General Menu. Serve cheeses and cold cuts cut with a bell-shaped cookie cutter. (Try to say that sentence three times fast!) Bake bell-shaped cookies in different flavors — chocolate chip, sugar, any kind of dough that can be rolled and cut. Prepare stuffed bell peppers for your main course.

Favors

Place a memento bell in crystal, china, or metal in a gift bag with some chocolate, foil-wrapped bells.

If this party is bell-low you and your friends, why don't you try . . .

A Silver Bell Ball

The formal version of the Jingle Bell Bash. Basically, the same thing but much more silver and stuffiness.

Invitations

Silver paper cut in the shape of bells or real silver bells. Place in a gift bag or box with party information and fill with strands of silver tinsel.

Attire

Simply silver spoonish. Or, snooty snobbish.

Decorations

General Christmas with more silver than usual. Hang and place garlands, tinsel, and bowls of ornaments here and there. Tie silver lamé bows to chair backs. Drape silver lamé cloths over table tops. Add plenty of white lights and mirrors. Use silver serving pieces. (*See* Silk Stockings Hung from the Mantle Without Care party for additional ideas.)

Menu

General Christmas. Serve swordfish and other silver food, such as Hershey Kisses. Any food served in silver serving pieces is perfect.

Favors

Give your guests recordings of "Silver Bells." A beautiful silver plated mirror, candy dish, ornament, or trinket box are lovely gifts and are relatively inexpensive at discount chains such as TJ Maxx and Marshall's.

If you believe only a ding dong would throw this party, why don't you try . . .

Chapter ☀11

Bake-☆Offs

A lot of people think the word "baking" is the same as the word "holiday." When the "h" word is first whispered, recipes are exchanged and cookie sheets are counted. Ingredients are inventoried and shopping and gift lists are made. That's just the way it is. Many holiday memories are triggered at the twitch of a nose catching a whiff of freshly baked gingerbread and spice cake. Food plays a lead role in the seasonal show. This chapter suggests a few ways to turn the usual foodstuffs into an unusual event, all done in good taste (hopefully).

Fruitcake Fling

Ah . . . finally, a use for the ubiquitous fruited brick. Just fling it! (Free legal advice: Look before you fling — if someone gets hurt, you may have to shell out some big bucks — it could seriously impact your partying budget.)

Invitations

If you are brave, send the party information wrapped around a fruitcake. (It's okay to use the ones you've been stockpiling over the years. I suggest using cakes that are no more than three years old. Do not, I repeat, do not, go back any farther.) If you don't have your own stash, use store-bought cakes. A potholder with the party information on it is also a creative way to ask your friends over. Ask your guests to bake a fruitcake using their favorite recipe and bring the cake and the recipe to the party.

Attire

Nutty as a fruitcake frocks.

Decorations

Your General Christmas will do. The highlight will be the table for the fruitcake display. Try to make it look marvelously appetizing (quite the challenge).

Menu

Man (and woman) can't survive on fruitcake alone so you'll have to offer your guests something else to chomp on. Make your selection from The Cake. You can always separate the fruit from the cake and offer fresh fruit and a variety of cakes. The real production will occur when your guests' cakes are unveiled. Serve the fruited bricks with a coffee bar, stocked with a really strong brew and equally strong liqueurs. It's amazing how sipping "special" coffees enhances the "flavor" of the fruitcake immensely.

Favors

There are many bake-off categories you can come up with — most tasteful, most tasteless, heaviest, most fruit, most nuts, most creative, most odd shaped. The bake-off winners receive holiday cookbooks. Give personalized aprons to all your guests, or potholders, oven mitts, and dish towels.

If you can deal with an all nutty party or an all fruity one but not both, why don't you try . . .

Get Stewed!

Next in the series of bake-off gatherings is the winter stew competition.

Invitations

Pot holders can be used to transmit the invitations. Or, attach the party information to a packet of stew seasoning, or send over a can of stewed tomatoes and ask your guests to start from there. Ask your guests to bring a pot of their famous stew.

Attire

Stew style. Just throw something together.

Decorations

Create a down-home, comfy feeling. Simmer oranges, cinnamon sticks, and cloves on the stovetop (make sure you put these ingredients in a pot with some water before placing on the burner!) Put clove studded oranges in a bowl. Use red and white checked napkins and tablecloths. Carve out pumpkins and different kinds of squash to use as "bowls" for the stews. Scatter branches of evergreen over the serving table and around the serving pieces. Place candles everywhere (in spice or country apple scent).

Menu

You'll want to make your own stew and offer it with your guests' creations. Put out an assortment of homemade breads and country biscuits in napkin lined baskets. Add some flavored butters in crock pots. Before the stew contest begins, you might want to have a tray of assorted cheese and crackers and sausages and mustards. Dessert can be strawberry shortcake or warm fruit cobbler served with a scoop of cinnamon ice cream.

Favors

Award cookbooks to the winners in different categories — best overall, thickest, heartiest, most ingredients. Recipe cards and pens, aprons, chef's hats, pot holders, mitts, and dish towels also make great prizes and mementos.

If your idea of getting stewed has nothing to do with cooking in the kitchen, why don't you try . . .

Mrs. Claus's Co-Ed Cookie Dis-Connection

Mrs. Claus has had enough. Being the perfect little (okay, not that little) wife season after season after season. Cooking 17 meals a day for her husband. Bathing all those little elves (glue, paint, and wood shavings in places you can't even imagine!). And those reindeers! Scooping up by the bucketful! She's fed up and isn't going to take it anymore. Things are going to be different in North Pole this year — why not be a part of it? You and your guests will disconnect all the negative people, places, and things from your lives, and you'll do it with cookies. (Big tip: To minimize the risk of offending a guest, make sure your guests know who else has been invited!)

Invitations

Put the dry ingredients to make sugar cookies in a shopping bag with the party information written on a recipe card. Include a basic sugar cookie recipe and ask your guests to make a couple of jumbo size cookies from one batch and to decorate them with frosting and icing words and designs representing people, places, or things they'd love to get out of their lives. Ask your guests to bring their cookie creations to the party.

Attire

Liberating look. Shed your aprons and sources of stress.

Decorations

An eclectic mix of General Christmas and modern North Pole kitchen complete with the aroma of cookies and gingerbread (from scented candles). Place an assortment of fresh baked breads and pies (still packed in the bakery boxes they came in) on the kitchen counters. Have a copy of the December issue of *Clausmopolitan* magazine on the kitchen counter opened to the page where Mrs. Claus's article *101 Ways to Drive Your Man Crazy In Red With Some Milk and Cookies* appears. Pile up three weeks worth of laundry in the corner. Leave a stack of dishes in the sink and top with a few sprigs of holly.

Menu

General Christmas. Offer lots of liberating libations. Dessert is served when your guests are ready to disconnect. Here's how to do it. Bring on the "stressfully" decorated cookies and DEVOUR. Wash down with assorted coffees. There you have it. You've gotten rid of all the kinks in your life. (We all wish it was this easy — eat a few cookies and BAM! No more troubles. We can only hope, and isn't that what the season is all about anyway?)

Favors

Present Christmas cookie cookbooks, or a subscription to *Cosmopolitan* and *Better Homes & Gardens* (for him) to your guests.

If you've been devouring cookies by the dozens for years and not a darn thing has changed except for your waist line, why don't you try . . .

Chapter ❄ 12

Drinking

Just as baking is a big part of the holidays as mentioned in the previous chapter, drinking is also one and the same during the festive season. I'm not suggesting that the only way to have fun at a party is to drink "real" drinks, however, it's a fact of life that partiers just might be looking for a libation or two. I'm not encouraging the consumption of alcohol, however, just in case your definition of a good drink includes some, you may be interested in the five very alive parties on the pages to follow. Of course, you can certainly modify the ideas by leaving the alcohol off your shopping list. You know your guests and what kind of party you want to have. The only modification that shouldn't be made — ever — is the desire to have a great time. Party on!

Frothy the Snowman

The real story behind our favorite little snowman.

Invitations

Write the party information on to white paper cut in the shape of a snowman. Place in a clear vellum envelope, add some silver and white confetti and snowflakes. Or, glue cotton balls onto the snowman-shaped card and decorate it to look like a snowman. Write the party information on the back, place in an envelope, and send off.

Attire

Showy snowman (or woman). White clothes accessorized with black top hats (which can be found in a costume or party supply store), mufflers, carrot noses, and coal eyes.

Decorations

General Christmas. Plug in a "Frosty the Snowman" video. Check out snow-making ideas in Ski Bunnies — Oops! Wrong Holiday, I Mean Ski Funnies — Aprés Ski WHEEEEE! party. Build a snowman or two to place near the keg of beer using Styrofoam™ balls and cotton or poly fiber fiberfill (quilting material). Arm yourself with a hot glue gun and assemble the snowy creature. Glue the Styrofoam™ balls together to form a larger ball shape — making three balls as large as you want to. Glue the three balls together to form a snowman. Cover with the fiberfill and spray all over with artificial snow. Glue on coal eyes and mouth and carrot nose — top with a hat and muffler, lean a broom on him (with any luck, one of your guests may take the hint and sweep the kitchen floor).

Menu

General Christmas. Add some "frothy" stuff. Beer comes to mind — and lots of it! (Now you know the real scoop on Frosty!) Put cans and bottles of beer in a large container — a half barrel works well and looks good — and load with lots of frosty ice. Make sure to have non-alcoholic brews and other beverages available, such as root beer. Slap on a "Frosty's Froth" label to the side of a keg of beer. Serve bowls, baskets, and platters of carrots and coal (dark chocolate anything), beer nuts, beer bread, and hot dogs steamed in beer.

Favors

Give each of your guests a top hat and a cornhusk pipe or a "Frothy Snowman" etched glass mugs filled with beer nuts and wrapped in cellophane tied with a plaid bow. Offer contest prizes such as *Frosty the Snowman* books and videos and for whoever sings "Frosty the Snowman" the best (or the worst).

If too much froth melts you, why don't you try . . .

The Little Rummer Boy

The time Bacardi® beat out the Energizer® batteries. It kept beating, and beating, and beating.

Invitations

Tiny drums, of course! Write the party information on the top or the side of the drum. Place the drum in a box filled with straw and deliver with a pair of real drumsticks. (Yes, the drum and the sticks won't be in proportion — they're simply tokens and for fun). Or, tie the party information around the neck of a miniature bottle of rum, place the bottle in a straw-filled brown paper bag, close with a ribbon, and deliver.

Decorations

General Christmas with more drums than usual. Turn drums upside down and use as serving pieces. Hire a band with an awesome drummer. Invite a "pirate, rum-bottle swigging" Santa to "Ho Ho Ho and a bottle of rum" your guests.

Menu

Look through the suggestions in Chapter One. Prepare rum-flavored recipes, of course, such as rum balls and rum cake. Serve chicken and/or turkey "drumsticks" and bread sticks. Serve assorted rum drinks — on the rocks and frozen. Pour plenty of Rummer Boys.

Favors

Have a talent contest — who can sing "The Little Drummer Boy" the best, the worst, and in the most creative way wins a prize. Or have a gin rummy contest. Bottles of rum and Energizer batteries make novel favors and prizes. Bottles of analgesic labeled "Little Rummer Boy Remedy" to help those pounding heads and bags of butter rum candies are also appropriate mementos.

If rum causes more headaches than the sound of that little drum, why don't you try . . .

Not a Pretty Sight: the Morning After

This is a party out-of-necessity and is necessarily very easy to pull together.

Invitations

A bottle of analgesics in a little bag that includes the party information. Or, staple a packet of hangover powder you can pick up at the drugstore or liquor store, single dose sizes of analgesic and Alka Seltzer® to printed invitations. "Take 2 and join us in the morning."

Attire

Same style. Whatever you wore the night before is just fine. Come on over wearing whatever you had on when you spilled out of bed this morning (please, at least a robe). This is another "who-cares" party, so dressing right should be the last thing on anyone's mind.

Decorations

Extreme peace and quiet. Place lots of aspirin bottles around the party area.

Menu

The "menu" begins with Bloody and Virgin Marys. Have a variety of mixes — regular tomato juice, Mr. & Mrs. T's in mild and spicy, clamato juice. Stock up on some good vodka (really, really good). Don't forget the garnishes — crisp, leafy celery stalks, green olives, cocktail onions, cucumber spears. Set up some extras for a zing — horseradish, Tabasco sauce, and any other type of liquid fire. Now for the food. How about a bagel bar? Bagels, otherwise known as "life preservers" during heavy-headed times, are great energy sources, especially when chased by a spicy Bloody Mary. Buy an assortment of cream cheese, some bagels and lox, sliced tomatoes and onions, capers, crumbled egg yolks, and caviar. Put out a variety of jellies and jams. Add some muffins and pastries and you'll be ready for your guests to pour in.

Favors

The favor has already been done — the Bloodys have been poured and the life preservers have been tossed (hopefully in the good way). However, if you'd still like your friends to leave with a memento, how about some more aspirins in a gift bag? You can also throw in a refrigerator magnet printed by a taxi company that has their telephone number, just in case.

If you have no idea where you are or how this book got into your hands, why don't you take two aspirins, call your doctor in the morning, recuperate, resuscitate, and rejuvenate then try . . .

No-Whine Wine Tasting

No doubt the holidays are a hectic time of the year. The time of the year when complaints galore are voiced. We hear about long lines, late deliveries, slow cashiers, rude salespeople, slow drivers, season traffic, and the price of tea in China. Ironically, the complaints usually roll off the tongues of the people who have waited until the very last minute to do whatever needs to be done. I say, quit the whining and keep things in perspective. One way to do this is by hosting a "no-whine" wine party. A couple or more hours where things just don't matter and complaints aren't welcome. You're breathing and that's cause for a celebration. If you aren't convinced, here's another reason for this party. Legend has it that the original Rudolph the Red-Nosed Reindeer had nothing to do with a freak baby deer with a funky nose that glows. Here's the story. Baby Rudolph's condition was inherited from his great-great grandfather, Rudy, who led a thousand drunken sailors across holiday-hectic waters in hope of reuniting with their families in time for the holidays. Rudy was honored (basically stuck) with this job not because he was a natural born leader. Not because he was a navigable water whiz. Nothing like that at all. Rudy took the helm because he had so much to drink causing his nose to turn red and glow, as bright as a light bulb on Bourbon Street. He was the only one who could lead (scary, huh?) But hey, who's complaining? All those men and boys made it home. I know it's a touching story, however, don't take out the hanky. Nope. Take out a bottle of Merlot. (Rumor has it that Rudy favored Merlot). In honor of the real red-nosed deer, quit the whining and enjoy!! Here's to you, Rudy. Cheers!

Invitations

Bottles of cheap red wine that have the party information on the label. Place in a brown paper bag, throw in a bag of sour cherry drops, twist at the neck, and tie with a jute string.

Attire

Wine wear with a holiday nautical flare. Don't complain that you don't have a thing to wear! Dig out that cabernet-stained silk blouse you've been holding on to from that important client dinner at your boss' home when that bottle "oops, it slipped" from your hand (perhaps you can borrow your boss' shirt or the client's blazer — go for whatever is the most stained).

Decorations

General Christmas. Put candles in top of empty wine bottles (assorted) and place throughout the party area. Wine label napkins, coasters, and corks can be used.

Menu

Serve assorted wines (chardonnay, merlot, zinfandel, dessert, sparkling), cheese (brie, camembert, gouda, muenster), wine, crackers (wheat biscuits, flaky, sesame, pepper), wine, bread (French, Italian, sour dough), wine, fruit (grapes, strawberries, wedges of apple and pear), wine, hors d'oeurves (shrimp, paté, stuffed mushroom caps, toast points with caviar), wine, desserts (chocolate dipped strawberries, white chocolate mousse cake), and . . . some wine. Group food and wines that compliment each other. Print 2-inch by 3-inch cards with wine information: Name, country, years, special notes. White wine should be chilled for two hours before serving. Open red wine an hour before to allow time to breathe. Label cheese with tiny markers to identify what it is. I've seen them in porcelain and wood. You'll know your brie from your gouda and your muenster from your parmesan. Everyone will be impressed.

You can do dessert and wine, too. Pair sweetened cheeses with pound cake, date bread, and gingersnaps. Havarti cheese tastes great on graham crackers. Slice bite-size pieces of the cakes and breads right before your guests arrive to avoid the cakes from drying out.

Favors

Present bottles of holiday specialty wine such as Blizzard Burgundy. They can be found at better department or liquor stores. Offer guides to wine-tasting, "No whining" buttons, corkscrews, and wine bottle stoppers. Your guests won't whine when you send them home with a wine glass filled with candy and wrapped in a cellophane square with the edges brought together at the top and tied with a fancy gold and burgundy ribbon.

If you feel Merlot has got to go and Chardonnay only gets in the way, find your own way to glow by trying . . .

Redneck Christmas Rally

Forget that red-nosed reindeer, what about the rednecks? They're always ready to party. There will be a special appearance by Jack "Daniels" Frost to do some "nipping at your nose".

Invitations

A miniature bottle of Jack Daniels® with a muffler tied around the neck of the bottle and a mini Santa hat on top (miniature hats can be found at any dime store during the holidays — if you can't find them, alter a miniature Christmas stocking). Place in a box (ah . . . a Jack in the box) with the party information. Sprinkle with artificial snow and send it on its merry way.

Attire

Lumberjack happy sack. Tennessee drinking togs. Wear flannel shirts and jeans, cowboy boots, cowboy hats or Budweiser logo caps, chewing tobacco, and overalls. Anything made out of denim, gingham, and saddle leather will fit right in.

Decorations

General Christmas with A Christmas Round-Up: Yee Ha! and Ho Ho Ho! Hoedown party suggestions.

Menu

Down home Southern Christmas cooking. Serve macaroni and cheese, baby back ribs, black-eyed peas and rice, collard greens, chicken fried steak and gravy, corn bread and fresh butter, and some homemade biscuits and gravy. Dessert is a warm peach cobbler and an apple pie with a scoop of homemade vanilla ice cream. You'll be dishing out some good old-fashioned Southern comfort.

Or, if you're not up to real Southern hospitality (you'd much rather mingle with Jack), pick up some Jack-in-the Box® fast food if you're lucky enough to have one in your neck of the woods. Order a feast from the comfort of your car. When the Jack-in-the-Box welcomes you with "May I take your order, please?" Go for it. If you don't have this luxury, serve up some quick fixin's such as Monterey Jack cheese on saltines, Jackpot stew shell (heat up some canned stew) served in a carved out jack-o-lantern, or Applejack pie (heat up a frozen apple pie). Serve sweet potato jackets with maple syrup (zap some potatoes in a microwave, scoop out the insides, drizzle with syrup), and corn bread and butter. Pour Jack Daniels with coke, Jack Daniels with tonic and lime, Jack Daniels with 7-Up, and the happy holiday hour special: Jack Daniels with cranberry juice and a splash of lime, otherwise known as "the Jackhammer".

Favors

Your guests will be delighted with a *Southern Living* magazine (the Christmas issue is fantastic), a belt buckle with their name on it, or a copy of Jeff Foxworthy's, *You Know you're a Redneck When . . .* book.

If you're just too jack tired to pull this one off, why don't you try . . .

Chapter 13

Games

Look no further if you want to keep your guests involved with each other. The next few party ideas have your guests playing games and working on group projects. I know, I know! It sounds like a day at the office, however, rest assured, the ideas you'll find here are positive experiences and no one gets hurt! Your guests will be invited to take a few chances, legitimately earn some funny money, become contortionists, and grab a few pieces. Innocent fun, but fun nonetheless, and lots of it. It's play-party time! So, without further ado, close your eyes, turn yourself around a few times, and pin the guest list on a party!

Have a Very Merry Christmas: Wanna Bet!?

No, this isn't Scrooge revisited. It's an evening full of fun and excitement as Santa brings the adults games they really want to play! You know, blackjack, craps, roulette, and a slot machine or two, to name a few.

Invitations

Printed invitations with a few poker chips or slot machine tokens rolled into the envelopes like a pair of loaded dice before sealing. Or, attach the party information to a deck of cards or to a pair of those rearview mirror fuzzy dice in red or green.

Attire

Las Vegas glitz.

Decorations

General Christmas with more lights than usual (neon?).

Menu

Think junket. Gamblers are usually treated to a "luscious" smorgasbord to whet their appetite for get-rich-quick possibilities with a one armed bandit. Recreate the gambling spread by serving platters of cold cuts, deli salads, cheese slices, mustards, mayos, breads and rolls, pickle chips, tomato and onion slices, and lettuce leaves. Serve all the makings of mobster, I mean monster, hero sandwiches. Offer real quick bites so your guests can get back to pulling the slots and rolling the dice.

Favors

All the top "winners" get prizes such as books on a relevant topic: "How To Make Big Bucks Gambling", "Black-market Secrets To

Blackjack", and "How To Pull A Jackpot Slot Every Time!" (These aren't real titles, however, I'll bet that you can find some very similar at the bookstore). Send everyone home with a deck of cards and a scorepad.

If all bets are off on this one, why don't you try . . .

Don't Be Bored, Get Out the Board!

If playing games is right up your alley, this party is for you. You and your guests will enjoy Monopoly®, Trivial Pursuit®, Jeopardy®, Twister®, Candy Land®, and Chutes and Ladders® challenges. The purpose is to take a well-deserved break during the holidays — to make time for nothing but fun and games for a change!

Invitations

Print invitations in the form of a Trivial Pursuit card (Q: Best party of the season. A: The Smith's Q: Where do the Smith's live? A: 32 Oak Street Q: What time does the party start? A: 8:00 p.m. give or take a few minutes) or attach party information to some Monopoly money (Pass Go, Collect $200, Avoid Jail . . . Go to the Smith's house). It depends on what games you have in mind.

Attire

Game gear. Wear sit-on-the-floor comfortable clothes or something capable of being twisted, if that's the gig for the evening.

Decorations

General Christmas with tokens of the game you're playing. Centerpieces can have Trivial Pursuit cards on sticks placed in the dirt of a plant or some Monopoly money floating on some greenery with lights and garland. Candy Land is easy (I feel my creative juices start to wake up . . . how about sprinkling some candy across the table? Now that's an idea.)

Menu

Fun, fun, fun. Think of amusement parks. Serve cotton candy, hotdogs, soft pretzels, peanuts, popcorn, candy apples, and fried dough — just about anything that'll make you sick if you eat too much of it.

Favors

Have a travel size version of whatever game you've played for each of your guests to take home.

If boards bore you (game boards that is, not as in Board of Directors, Certification Board, or Board of County Commissioners), why don't you try . . .

Find A Piece, Get Some Peace

Are you looking for a piece? If so, you're at the right place. Get a piece of the holiday action — a jigsaw puzzle piece that is.

Invitations

For each guest, buy small (about 5-inch by 5-inch) puzzles from a card, toy, craft, or party store, either in plain white or seasonal design. Put the puzzle together, turn it over, and write the party information on the back. Break up the pieces and place in an envelope and toss in some Christmas confetti. (If you're using plain white puzzles, the party information is to be written on the front of the puzzle and then decorated). Your guests will have to put the puzzle together to find out what's going on and where.

Attire

Sit-on-the-floor-or-around-the-table holiday casual.

Decorations

General Christmas. Scatter puzzle pieces on the serving table with some confetti. Set up a table where the action will take place (perhaps the kitchen or the dining room). A coffee table will also work. Your guests can sit around it on floor cushions. Buy a Christmas theme jigsaw puzzle. Hallmark stores usually have a good selection. The challenge will be to put the puzzle together during the party. No one can leave until it's done. (What? Is the Godfather Santa returning?) The finished product is then sealed and donated to a nursing home or shelter.

Menu

General Christmas. Serve "food" that can be pieced together like a puzzle such as pizza, cake, or some cookies. For example, roll out cookie dough and form a square or rectangle. Trim the edges so they are even. Using a pizza cutter, roll the blade across the dough, cutting connecting shapes (imagine you're cutting a puzzle). Move the pieces slightly to allow them to bake separately. Bake per recipe and voila! A cookie puzzle.

Favors

Your guests will enjoy crossword puzzle books, pens, crossword dictionaries, and jigsaw puzzles to work on at home.

If you can't see how this piece party will bring you peace, in fact, you felt you were misled on this one from the beginning, why don't you try . . .

Chapter ☼ 14

Hit the Road

The parties in this chapter have you and your guests taking road trips in personal or chartered vehicles to all sorts of exciting destinations. There's a wide (and wild) world out there and the sky is the limit (which reminds me, airplanes are also appropriate modes of transportation). Get out and about and expand your own horizons with any one of the next five parties. You and your guests will be whisked off to a broadway production, a ballet, or my favorite place — the mall — all the while spreading and discovering holiday cheer via their own wheels, someone else's, or by foot. It's time to walk and roll in the name of FUN! And let's make a big production of it, leading us right in to the first party of this chapter.

The Bus Stops Here

Hop in a bus, van, car, or suitable vehicle for a road trip to a Christmas play, musical, choir production, or some other holiday event. Find out what's going on in your area and reserve seating/tickets for you and your guests. The most popular productions during the holidays are *The Nutcracker* ballet, *The Messiah*, and *A Christmas Carol*.

Invitations

Get a playbill, flyer, or brochure describing the event you selected. Use a hole punch and make a hole in the upper left hand corner of what you're working with. Thread a ribbon through the hole and tie into a bow. Or, create simulated tickets to the planned event with all the party information printed on it. If you're going to a musical, attach the party information to miniature French horn ornaments.

Attire

Appropriate for the event — let your guests know.

Decorations

General Christmas.

Menu

If you've arranged for your guests to meet at your house before the event, serve cocktails and hors d'oeuvres. If after, coffee and dessert. You could also prepare snacks-in-a-box for each of your guests and pack a cooler of beverages for the ride depending on how far you must travel. If you're chartering a vehicle, check with the bus company to see if there are any restrictions.

Favors

Offer your guests a cassette, videotape, or other memento of what you saw presented in a holiday gift bag.

If it's a heck of a lot easier on yourself to sleep at home rather than in the theater and to not have to go through all this just to catch a few winks, why don't you try . . .

Hip Hop Shop 'Til You Drop

Be hip. Hop on over to the mall and onto Santa's lap, and tell him what you want for Christmas. Don't be shy.

Invitations

Attach party information to a map of a mall with great Christmas shopping. Outlets are favorites and every one that I've been to (and there have been many) provide maps showing you what shops are there and where. You might want to include a shopping list notepad with a Christmas theme, and a holiday pen or pencil. Place all in shopping bags (a great way to recycle the bags you may be accumulating — I have enough for at least 207 guests as my husband will tell you).

Attire

Very merry mall.

Decorations

This is easy, depending on your plans. Your General Christmas will be fine. Tie balloons to the handles of shopping bags that you have weighted down with a mug to keep it upright (more good uses for your shopping bag stash).

Menu

Have everyone meet at your house before you head to the mall for an all day spree. Some mimosas, bagels, muffins, danishes, and coffee will provide your guests the needed shopping stamina. After your splendid day, have a "hip hop happy hour" back at your house, giving all the power shoppers a chance to unwind. Serve a special drink such as the Hip Hop Shop Slop or Shop Poppers (a shooter). There's nothing magical about this drink-of-the-day as far as creativity goes other than what you call it. Simply mix your favorite cocktail, shooter, or both, and give them new names. You could also set up a tea or coffee bar.

Favors

Your guests will appreciate a bottle of peppermint foot lotion to rub on their tired tootsies. The Body Shop and Garden Botanika make excellent lotions. Or gift wrap a frame for each of your guests to hold their photo with Santa-at-the-mall.

If you've already dropped from shopping, and your hip hop is a flop, why don't you try . . .

Hey, Hey, Hey What a Sleigh!

The way you get to this party is the focus. Each of your guests are to decorate their cars (hereinafter referred to as "sleighs" for the unlimited purpose of this party). Think of how much holiday cheer will be spread while your guests drive to your party. (Not to mention the stares). Encourage each guest to decorate their car, truck, bike, van, skateboard, in-line skates, etc. in the holiday spirit. (Free legal advice: If using public transportation — check with your local authority. Some restrictions may apply, including, but not limited to, a prohibition on the attachment of reindeer horn hood ornaments to a bus and the painting of its tires green and red).

Invitations

Make phony driver's licenses using a photograph of Santa and appropriately place the party information. (More free legal advice: Don't try to pull a fast one on the Division of Motor Vehicles — they have ways of making you talk, which usually results in you having to walk the rest of your life if you don't have a license to drive.) Attach party information to a wreath that you'll ask each guest to put on the grill of the vehicle they're taking to get to the big party. You could also attach the party information to tiny sleigh ornaments and place in a box or a bag with shredded tissue paper.

Attire

What your guests wear isn't as important as what their ride wears. Any clothes will do but all driving guests and passengers are to wear Santa caps or reindeer horns (these can be ordered through many catalogs or can be found at a pet shop — it's okay to buy them there, no one has to know they were intended for a thirty pound cat). Battery-operated lights can easily decorate the sleigh. How about some garland on that luggage rack? Or how about replacing that plastic daisy on your antenna with a ball of holly? (you'll still be able to find your car in the mall parking lot.)

Decorations

General Christmas is all you need indoors. You need to put your creative energy into the sleigh parking lot. Post "Sleigh Parking Only" signs. Rope off with garland and twinkling lights. Place buckets of reindeer feed for the hungry creatures (use birdseed).

Menu

Truck stop slop. Fuel your guests tanks with greasy spoon stuff! The kind of food we all love even though one meal makes up our weekly allowance of fat grams (that's why the fixin's taste so darn good). This is a great party to do as a brunch or breakfast. Serve steak and eggs with tons of ketchup, hash browns, and grits. Offer eggs over easy with a pound of crispy bacon and corned beef hash. Pour mugs of strong coffee. Set up an "auto parts supply" smorgasbord. Serve doughnuts and bagels (hey, hey, hey sleigh wheels) and fillers (more than air because it's Christmas, such as cream cheese), nuts (all kinds), "grill"ed food, with the "tools" being the utensils.

Favors

Have prizes for the best sleigh, most festive, least-spirited, biggest, and smallest. Present gift certificates for lube jobs, tire rotations, and sleigh washes and waxes. Driving gloves are also nice. Everyone leaves with a bottle of car wash and a can of oil (actually a bottle of olive oil with the label changed).

If you recently had a lube and rotation and aren't due for another this season, why don't you try . . .

Clueless Seasonal Sightings

This one goes all over town. Your guests will have fun searching for holiday items.

Invitations

Each guest receives the party information on the back of a scavenger hunt map. The map includes a list of holiday treasures with an itsy bitsy clue (basically clueless) as to where that treasure may be found. For example, "Go to a place known for it's caroling parrots." Ah ha! Your guests will know that Pancho's Pub is known for their singing birds and they'll head there. The site of the tallest tree in the city, the store with the most festive decorations, a bar with three wreaths on each window. Think of all that's going on where you live. You check out the holiday stuff, have libation, and head to the next spot. Make sure you have a designated driver. It's a lot cheaper to hire a car or limo and split the cost with your friends than the alternative.

Attire

Cool clued cop: A trench coat, a cockatoo for your shoulder, a pair of mirrored sunglasses, and a box of doughnuts. Think Dick Tracy.

Decorations

General Christmas at your home — everyone will meet there at the beginning and at the end of the hunt. Your guests will have to bring something back from each place they stopped at — a matchbook, napkin, business card, shopping bag, a barstool, the hostess, or the cute waiter.

Menu

Even though you'll be snacking at the sites, pack some food and drink to take with you on the road. When you return, have plenty of doughnuts for the hungry and tired detectives.

Favors

Give your guests Dick Tracy comic books, videos, or soundtracks, secret decoder rings, plastic water guns, or Clue®, the game.

If you haven't a clue how to pull this one off, (even with the game) why don't you try . . .

Ding Dong, Evan Calling!

Not the Avon lady, but close. Evan is an elf who goes door to door admiring others goodies and leaving some of his own, too. This is a great way to share your decorations with others. Plan a Christmas spirit tour. Check out trees and collectibles such as Dickens Villages, Snow Villages, and others by Department 56. Some people collect ornaments, some just go crazy with outdoor decorations. People love to check out, admire and compare what other people collect, especially if they're into the same things. Show off what you're known for.

Invitations

Put the party information on the back of a tour map. Use whatever symbolizes the tour mission. For example, if it's trees you're checking out, tie a cutting of evergreen with a plaid ribbon or put a strand of lights or a single lightbulb in a bag or box if you're going gaga over light displays.

Attire

Comfortable touring togas.

Decorations

The decorations are whatever decorations the houses on the tours have. Make sure every destination has their special display highlighted. Each site will decorate their serving table to reflect their collection.

Menu

Everyone meets at the first stop and has some snacks and drinks before heading over to the next. Each stop will have some sort of treat, beginning with cocktails and hors d'oeuvres and progressing to the last stop for dessert. Serve something consistent with your exhibit. For example, if you have a Santa collection you're sharing, offer some cookies cut in the shape of Santa, or use plates and napkins patterned with Santas, or use Santa caps to hold utensils.

Favors

Each stop can provide a memento. For example, back to the Santa collection, a personalized Santa ornament for each guest. For a light display, give each guest a candle in any luscious holiday scent.

If the only collection you have is a jar full of your baby teeth (each and every one), why don't you try . . .

Chapter ☼15

Christmas Fever: Hot! Hot! Hot! In the Cold! Cold! Cold!

This chapter features polar opposites. The cold meeting the hot. You don't need a beach for a beach party and you don't need snow for a snow party. If you're snowed in, and you tell your mind that you'd rather be at the beach, your strong desire to be there will spark your imagination and you'll create that environment. Likewise, if you're a victim of humidity, you might imagine yourself making angels in the snow. Please, don't let anything stop you from having the party YOU want! Not even acts of God or Weaver the Weatherman.

Beach Blanket Gift Wrap

I'll start this section off with a party full of my passion — the sun, the sea, and the sand. You don't need to live in a seaside villa or a warm climate to enjoy this one. In fact, it's more fun to do this party if you have snow outside your artificial palm fronded windows. Just use your imagination. Pretend you're in Tahiti and you will be. Don't let reality get in the way of bringing sunshine and good cheer to your friends during the holidays. Think beach bash! A summer picnic even though it's winter and 40° F below.

Invitations

Inflate beach balls and write the party information directly on them with a ball-point pen. Deflate the ball, stuff in an envelope, and mail. Another idea is to write the party information on a 3-inch by 5-inch plain index card (feel free to jazz it up), punch a hole in the upper left-hand corner of the card, thread a ribbon through the hole, and tie it to the arm of a pair of cheap sunglasses (red and green plastic frames). Place the sunglasses in a box full of sand, add some shells and a paper parasol, sprinkle with some artificial snow, and deliver.

Attire

Lazy days of summer (which could mean sweaters, winter coats, and long johns over your bathing suit depending on where you live).

Decorations

Set up and spread out beach umbrellas and blankets indoors or outdoors for your guests to sit under and on. Spray seashells and starfish red, green, and gold and place in various containers filled with sand. Suspend cutouts of fish in the party area. These can easily be made out of heavy poster board and brightly painted and hung with fishing line. Set up a sandbox, indoors and/or outdoors, and toss in some beach toys for your guests to play with. Play some Beach Boys Christmas tunes. Have a limbo contest (how low can you go?). Hire a steel drum band to move and groove your guests (make sure the band members wear Santa caps with their tropical print shirts). Ask guests to remove their shoes as they come through the door — have inexpensive beach thongs for them to wear.

Menu

Roll in a keg of beer (or two). Fill a kiddie swimming pool with ice and throw in some beers, sodas, and other beverages. Buy Styrofoam™ coolers and stencil or stamp with symbols of Christmas (stars and trees are good choices). Serve food in sand pails and use the shovels that usually come with them as serving pieces. Grill hot dogs and burgers indoors or outdoors with all the fixings. Don't forget the chips and dips. A clambake is also a great idea — throw a lobster, some clams, an ear of corn, and some red potatoes on a square of foil, drizzle with butter, and heat. Make sure all these items have been pre-cooked pursuant to cookbook suggestions — you're just reheating on the coals here.

Favors

Personalized sand dollar and seashell ornaments, beach towels, buckets, sunglasses, and beach toys are great take-homes from a day or night at the beach. Gift bags containing sample-size suntan lotion, oil, aloe vera gel, sunscreen, and lip balm are also nice souvenirs.

If a day at the beach has you seeing red (or feeling red), why don't you try . . .

Let It Snow! Let It Snow! And . . . Let It Snow!

This party makes quite an impact in places where snow isn't part of the holiday scene, such as in my home state of Florida.

Invitations

Snowflake cutouts with the party information written up and down the sides of the snowflake. Place in clear vellum envelopes with some iridescent snowflake-shaped glitter pieces with shreds of white and silver tinsel, into each envelope, and deliver. Or, bags of crushed ice (a.k.a. "snow") with the party information attached, delivered immediately.

Attire

Pure as the driven snow. Borderline flake.

Decorations

Spray pine cones white and finish with a spray of crystal glitter. Clear helium balloons imprinted with snowflake designs — as many as you can get — placed all over. 15-inch tissue paper snowflakes available from U.S. Toys (*See* the "Resources" section.) are great — suspend everywhere, using fishing line. Spray the windows on your house with artificial snow, even on the mirrors in the bathrooms and other glass surfaces in the party areas. Flocked Christmas trees are marvelously in accordance with the theme. Cover tables with silver lamé fabric and place a white organza or tulle square on top of it, cut large enough to drape over the sides of the table. An ice sculpture in the middle of the serving table will be a hit. Pink poinsettias, holly greens, and garlands of ivy strewn with silver Christmas balls, all add hints of color. Huge bows attached to the ends of curtain rods with trailing streamers in shimmery fabric make a nice flowing effect. Direct oscillating fans toward the streamers to create a winter breeze — swaying the gauze and other fabrics you've draped over the tables, windows, and furniture creating a winter wonderland. Place mirrors on the serving tables and spray with snow. You've heard of shower curtains, well how about snow curtains? Thread pieces of Styrofoam™ packing kernels on fishing line and hang strands of "snow" in your window (fill the entire opening). For the extravagant, rent a snow machine. Spray your guests' car windows with the same canned snow you used to decorate your house (Be careful: Don't block visibility — keep the snow off the windshield and the back window, and don't get any snow on the paint — it may damage the surface). There are many ways to fake snow. You can use cotton or polyester fiberfill to make snow drifts on table tops. Pull the fiberfill apart and lay it over the Styrofoam™ balls and blocks then spray with canned snow. (*See* Ski Bunnies — Oops! Wrong Holiday, I Mean Ski Funnies — Aprés Ski Wheeeee! party for more snow ideas.)

Menu

Serve only "white" food. Serve angel hair pasta with white clam sauce and fettucine alfredo. Prepare chicken and lobster, and some rice with diced green and red peppers. Go through your cookbooks for "white" food recipes for more ideas. Place chunks of fresh bread nearby in baskets. Serve devil's food cake hidden under mounds of fresh whipped cream, pound cake with marshmallow creme and angel food cake with assorted toppings. Offer fruit chunks served with melted white chocolate for dipping. Whip up some white chocolate snowflakes. Press melted white chocolate through a pastry bag onto a wax paper covered cookie sheet, drizzling the confection in snowflake shapes. Before it hardens, sprinkle with silver dragees. Chill. Simply peel off the paper when ready to use. As for drinks, serve clear ones — vodka, gin, tequila, rum, 7-UP, Sprite, and mineral water. Don't forget to mix up some of Fran's Reindeer Milk! (*See* Chapter One for the recipe.)

Favors

Have a crystal or sterling silver engraved ornament for each of your guests.

If the thought of snow sends a chill up and down your spine and has you reaching for your winter coat even if you live in the tropics (makes you wish you had a winter coat), why don't you try . . .

Island Christmas: Yo Mon!

Think of the contrast this party will have to the outdoors if you live in a dreary climate in the wintertime!

Invitations

Tie the party information to a red and green plastic lei or attach to a whole fresh pineapple placed in a crate or gift bag and delivered.

Attire

North Pole tropical. Put on a grass skirt with long underwear and boots if "temperaturely" required.

Decorations

Turn pineapples into Christmas trees by attaching tiny ornaments to the leaves using a hot glue gun (if real pineapples aren't available, silk or plastic ones will do). Put up a huge yellow shining sun (direct a bright light on it). Hand your guests red and green plastic or silk leis or have real ones made up using red and green carnations, with holly leaves alternating throughout. Place real or silk palm trees around and decorate with twinkling lights and ornaments. Hire an "island" Santa decked out in a Hawaiian shirt and dark sunglasses. Have a limbo contest — how low can you go? Color! Fun! Exotic! Tropical!

Menu

Serve roasted pig with all the fixings from your local butcher. Prepare jerk chicken, rice, and bowls of fresh fruit — a Caribbean feast. Blend some rum-runners and other holiday drinks — frozen concoctions of all kinds, topped with paper parasols. Serve in personalized souvenir hurricane glasses or pineapple or coconut shell halves. The sound of whirring blenders against a background of reggae Christmas music (cassette tapes, CD's, or a live steel drum band) sets the tone for a fun time.

Favors

Have prizes on hand for the lowest limbo-er. Gift bags of Kona coffee and macadamia nuts are a few tasty suggestions.

If you've already gone as low as you can and you'll never go there again, why don't you try . . .

Walking In a Winter Wonderland

A relaxing stroll around the neighborhood and back. Go through your neighborhood for an admire-the-decorations-stroll or head by foot to the town's Christmas tree lighting or a strip of shops that are known for their elaborate displays. Pick a destination and hit the pavement.

Invitations

Cut heavy paper in the shape of a boot. Use a hole punch where laces would go and then lace with real shoelaces in red, green, or a holiday design. Tie a jingle bell on each tip. Or, attach the party information to the cover of magazine on the subject of walking (such as *Walking* magazine available at your newsstand).

Attire

Bundle-up outdoor chic. Don't forget those boots that were made for walking (Nancy Sinatra comes to mind).

Decorations

Turn your party area into a winter wonderland. General Christmas and snow, snow, snow. Hang white twinkling lights everywhere. If you can find some bare tree branches, wrap with strands of twinkling white lights and place throughout the party area. "Plant" the branches in pots and vases, and place on a mantel or serving table as a centerpiece or in the bathroom (really cool in the shower — use battery-operated lights). Check out Ski Bunnies — Oops! Wrong Holiday, I Mean Ski Funnies — Aprés Ski Wheeeee! party for some more snow tips.

Menu

Serve snacks before you head out, with the big spread appearing after your walk. Check out The Cake for some ideas or Ski Bunnies

— Oops! Wrong Holiday, I Mean Ski Funnies — Aprés Ski Wheeeee! and Let it Snow! Let it Snow! And . . . Let it Snow! parties if you want to emphasize snow.

Favors

Hand out the current issue of *Walking* magazine, rolled and tied with a pair of shoelaces. Your guests will thank you for walking audio-tapes and books, coupons to a sporting goods store, or some thick cushiony socks.

If you'd rather kick back and yak rather than walk and talk, why don't you try . . .

Chapter 16

We're All the Same

In the previous chapter you were dealing with geographical differences. In this chapter, you have social differences. Country bumpkins meet Wall Street somethings. The point to be made is whether your idea of fun is sitting on the front porch chugging a can of beer or lounging on a chaise sipping a flute of Dom, we're all the same — wanting to take a load off, relax, do nothing except for what we want to do at the moment. And that includes partying at times. (Besides, too much beer or too much champagne makes all feel dull the next day!) This holiday season, forget what you are and think of who you are. If you're lucky, you'll be blessed with the wisdom that we're all the same after all where it matters. Here are a few parties on both sides, all in one chapter because all have one purpose — PARTY! Don't let technicalities stand in your way. Enjoy!

A Christmas Round-Up: Yee Haw!

For all you cowboys and cowgirls out there!

Invitations

A red bandanna with the party information written on it with a fabric pen or pinned to a corner. Fold and insert into a brown lunch-size paper bag, stuff with straw, and tie with a silver cord. Insert some wheat stalks into the cord's knot and dangle a red Christmas ornament bunch from the cord.

Attire

Christmas-in-the-city-slicker western.

Decorations

Regular Christmas decor westernized. Use haystacks for seats. Place decorated cacti throughout the house. They can be real or artificial — don't forget to string with lights. Anything western will do. If offered in or near your area, arrange for a hayride or a sleigh ride. Bring along wool blankets. Have a "western" Santa visit, laden with party favors for your guests.

Menu

Serve good ole barbeque, indoors or outdoors, depending on where you live or what you and your guests are willing to tolerate. We do it outside in the Sunshine State (unless the temperature dips below 70° F). Serve chili, corn bread, stick to your ribs ribs, chicken, corn on the cob, T-bone steaks, baked beans with brown sugar, pepper trays, and barbeque sauce galore (offer a selection). Use cowboy hats lined with red and green checkered napkins as serving pieces. Serve mugs of steaming hot chocolate with and without Peppermint Schnapps. Have a chili cook-off, rib contest, best barbeque sauce, and so on.

Favors

Give all your guests a straw cowboy hat with red and green plaid hat bands (glue a plaid ribbon in place with a hot glue gun). Pin on sheriff badges onto which you've glued a sprig of holly. Send guests home with a jar of chili mix with your favorite down home recipe attached, or bottles of your very own barbeque sauce (okay to buy at the grocery and re-label). (Free legal advice: You can relabel in the name of fun but you can't resell). Top the jars and bottles with a burlap square secured with a plaid ribbon.

If you've never been a Bonanza fan and don't own a 10 gallon hat and spurs for your boots (what!? No boots either?), why don't you try . . .

Ho Ho Ho! Hoedown

This is a more rough and ready type of Santa western party, not as genuine as A Christmas Round-Up: Yee Ha! party, if ya know what I mean. Git along little doggies!

Invitations

Pack the party information with a Santa ornament or figurine (preferably a Santa decked out in cowboy clothes) or have buttons that say "Santa Wants y'all!", imprinted with the party information on the back. Ask your guests to RSVP with a "Yee haw! I believe" or "No siree, I don't." Another idea is to stamp individual burlap bags with star shapes in red and green paint with a dash of glitter. Fill the bags with Santa candies and straw. Tuck party information inside, tie with jute string, and deliver horseback.

Attire

Country comfortable and jolly. Dress just a little square (if you're going to dance). Wear bib overalls.

Decorations

Imagine Santa relocating his headquarters to some small hick town far from the heart of Texas (somewhere near another organ) from the North Pole. Cowboy Claus negotiated a better economic development incentive package than he had hoped to. Yep, Pardner — the kind townsfolk gave him three six-packs and a bottle of Southern Comfort if he'd agree to grace their neck of the woods. If things don't work, Cowboy Claus could keep the generous liquids; however he would have to turn over "them thar deers for a mighty fine feast," if he did say so himself. Try to find one of those plastic life-size Santas that light up to place outside your front door to greet your guests and smaller versions to scatter throughout your house. Put cowboy hats and spurs on the Santas grazing, I mean gracing, your party. Go to the local watering hole and convince Cowboy Claus to drive his 4 x 4 to your home on the range and deliver party favors from his burlap sack, hooting and hollering "Ho Ho Ho Howdy Pardners! Merry Christmas to Y'all" Fill up the bed of a pick-up truck with some bales of hay and head to a country western bar to learn how to line dance. Have Cowboy Claus take you for a hayride (the hoe-down). Invite some square dancing elves to lead the party corner to corner and across the floor. Use cowboy hats turned upside down as serving pieces (be careful if using as a soup tureen — check with its owner first, as it may not be a purdy sight).

Menu

Serve cowboy grub. Check out A Christmas Round-Up: Yee Haw! party for ideas and then ring that triangle real good now, ya hear?

Favors

A red bandanna filled with tiny foil-covered chocolate Santas with the ends brought together at the top, and tied with a piece of calf-roping rope.

If you believe in St. Nick but have suspicions about this Cowboy Claus dude with the 4 x 4 pick-up truck, why don't you try . . .

Silk Stockings Hung from the Mantle Without Care

Christmas is spelled with 3 Big C's for this one: Caviar, Champagne, and Chocolate.

Invitations

You have a number of options here. You can go all the way and fill a small "silk" stocking (a regular Christmas stocking made from fancy fabric) with a split of champagne and an exquisite piece of chocolate. Write or print the party information on to an elegant piece of paper, roll and tie with a satin ribbon the color of champagne (ivory, ecru, beige), and place in the stocking. Or, you could put a spilt of champagne in a paper bag, drop in a few pieces of chocolate (Godiva® or Hershey Kisses are nice) with the party information tied to the neck of the bottle, asking your guests to wear silk to the party. You can write the party information right on to the bottle with one of those special glass-writing pens, which come in silver or gold ink. A small tin of caviar completes the whole silk stocking thing. Turn your party into a spoof on those stuffy formal affairs.

Attire

Black tie — real or really creative. Black tie "real" means tuxedos and ball gowns. Black tie "creative" means your guests must wear a black tie however and wherever they please.

Decorations

Float tons of balloons in white and ivory (champagne bubbles) throughout the party area. Tie them to the backs of chairs, to the middle of centerpieces, to anything that can anchor a helium balloon. Tie bunches of balloons to bottles of champagne and place throughout the party area. Tablecloths should be elegant — real fabric unless you're spoofing. Use real china and silver utensils. Rent silver serving and accent pieces: Candelabra, chafing dishes, tea sets, punch bowls, and other items to create a "rich" atmosphere. Don't forget the silk stockings. A few elegant Christmas stockings (real or improvised) hung on a mantel (without care — tossed to the wind and landed where they may) or in other areas is enough to bring the theme together. Use empty champagne bottles (ask a restaurant, club, or bar to save the empties for you) as candleholders by simply placing a taper candle in the opening and striking a match. Place on the serving table and other safe surfaces.

Menu

The menu is simply elegant hors d'oeuvres and savory finger food served in all those beautiful silver pieces you managed to gather. Serve champagne and mimosas in crystal flutes and passed around on a silver tray. Offer bowls of caviar served with toast points and delicate biscuits and chopped egg yolks and capers. Don't forget the chocolate or you'll never be forgiven. Truffles, tortes, mousses, and soufflés are excellent choices. Think dense and rich — luscious silky morsels to tantalize your guests' taste buds.

Favors

Give everyone a pair of silk socks or stockings stuffed in a Christmas stocking. A bottle of champagne adorned with a silk ribbon with your guests' names written or printed on the streamer or on the bottle will make quite an impression. Hand out a small box of Godiva chocolate. Anything homemade, especially when the recipe calls for champagne as the main ingredient, is delightful. These suggestions can also be used as the prizes for the most creative black tie or the most stuffy formal.

If the 3 C's of Christmas send you to the drugstore for Alka Seltzer Cold Medicine for those nasty stuffy head colds, or if your idea of a 3 C party is more like Cheerios, cola, and cheese puffs, why don't you try . . .

Christmas Smoke Screens

This party is in honor of all those people who smoked cigars way before it was the trendy thing to do. May they enjoy their pleasure forever, with the trendy ones moving on to the next "have to do because every one else does" movement.

Invitations

A big, fat cigar with the party information rolled around it like a tobacco leaf and loosely tied with a forest green ribbon. Or, a printed invitation with matchbooks stuck in the envelope before sealing.

Attire

Smoking jackets.

Decorations

General Christmas with a masculine touch. Think hunter green and plaid bows — smoky rooms. Create an atmosphere that reeks of big deals being cut. (I know, I know. Many women smoke the big one. If you're one of the stogie suckers, go ahead and do the feminine touch to the masculine thing). Hang cigars tied with ribbons on your Christmas tree.

Menu

This party is really an after-another-party party. Invite your guests to go back to your place for a good cigar and a smooth libation. Serve cordials, scotch, brandy, and martini's. You know — James Bond stuff. Food is optional. A few mixed nuts are plenty and so appropriate. One wouldn't want to ruin one's palate so as not to enjoy the taste of the smoke and delicious tobacco leaves. (Is it obvious that I'm a big cigar fan?)

Favors

Something very original and clever, like . . . a cigar! (Your guests can take one from your Christmas tree). Hand out rolls of breath mints and aerosol room sprays.

If smoking the big one isn't up your alley, why don't you try . . .

'Twas the Night Before Christmas and All Through the House, Everyone Was Stirring, Even the Mouse!

A martini party for all you stiff drinkers out there.

Invitations

Send an ornament in the shape of a house with an invitation to come stir with you.

Attire

Swizzle dazzle.

Decorations

General Christmas. Set up a martini bar. Make an olive tree to use as a centerpiece. Cover a Styrofoam™ cone with greenery. Put green olives on toothpicks and stick in to the tree. Intersperse Christmas ornaments with the olives.

Menu

General Christmas. Serve snacks that compliment martini's (may I suggest bowls of green olives and cocktail onions?) Martini's will be stirred, not shaken, sort of a reverse James Bond thing. Yep, we have it backwards and if we don't at the beginning, we'll surely have it that way at the end. Let's call it a 700 party. You have to offer 700 different types of martini's. (Only kidding, or not — it's your party). For your guests that don't indulge in this trendy drink, offer other beverages that are enhanced when stirred. Have an assortment of swizzle sticks.

Favors

Everyone departs with a jar of stuffed olives topped with a square of Christmas fabric, and tied with a jute string.

If you prefer to be shaken, not stirred, why don't you try . . .

Chapter ☀17

Grand Finale:
Desserts ☆Only

Well, the party is almost over. This is one I didn't want to end —
especially since dessert hasn't been served yet. The previous sixteen
chapters have led us each step of the way to the final sweet note, for
in this chapter, you'll discover a couple of real sweet parties that'll
send your guests sugar-high-tailing it home so you can start the party
clean up. (The time when the real fun begins.) These grand finale
parties are actually the main events, not mere endings to a full course.
Your guests will be delighted with your presentation of desserts and
only desserts. However, even though desserts are the only edibles
you'll be serving, your menu isn't limited. You'll also be serving fantasy. Add that delicious word to the "fun" that all parties must be and
you've created quite a potent pleaser. All your guests' senses will be
engaged — the sight of the luscious goodies, the aroma of the freshly baked delicacies, the taste (need I say more?), the various textures
and sensations you feel with eat, chew and, finally, the sound of the
"oohs" and "ahs" as the choice morsels are experienced. As the saying goes — "Aint' life sweet?" Yes it is. It's now time to remind your
guests of this truth and serve them some fantasy and fun with the
assorted flavors of the wonderful word: Dessert.

The Nutcracker Suite (Sweet)

A dessert only party! Inspired by the ballet.

Invitations

A wooden soldier nutcracker with a bag of sweets tied around its neck with the party information rolled into a scroll and tucked into the ribbon. Place the nutcracker in a gift box or bag with shredded tissue paper and a few whole nuts and deliver.

Attire

For the truly brave — "feel free to wear your favorite tutu." This one will surely separate the men from the boys. Mention that tutus will be available on site in case you "don't have time to pick up yours at the cleaners."

Decorations

The atmosphere should be fantasyland. Leaf through *The Nutcracker* ballet books for ideas. Capture the spirit. Sugar plum fairies abound! The lighting should be dim — dreamy. Drape lamp shades with large pastel-colored squares of tulle. Arrange a variety of nutcrackers everywhere. Fill bowls and baskets with assorted nuts still in the shell, begging to be cracked. Fill crystal bowls with sugar cubes (add food coloring to some to create a delicate tint). Use pastel serving pieces and containers, plates, and utensils (if using paper and/or plastic) and table coverings — casually drape double or triple layers of cloths of different colors on the table top. Play *The Nutcracker* soundtrack and/or rent the video of the production. If you know any ballerinas — your children, your friends' children or adults — bribe them to entertain your guests with a few twinkle-toe twirls and plie's. Have the dancers carry baskets filled with sweet treats to tantalize your guests. Locate a "ballerina" Santa (visualize this one!) or some *Nutcracker* characters from your local ballet company to mingle with your guests.

Menu

Serve desserts of every kind, stacked tall and spread wide. Recreate a candy shop feeling — a child's dream. "Plant" lollipop cookies on sticks into candy "dirt" (gumdrops) poured into white ceramic flower pots. Tie on a ribbon and bow and licorice strings. Make a gumdrop tree by poking gumdrops on the ends of a twig tree (buy at a craft store). Serve cakes with fluffy icing, sugar cookies frosted in pastel with sugar crystals dreamily sprinkled atop, and mountains of sugarplums (Trivia break: Did you know that sugarplums don't have plums in them? They are round or oval chocolates filled with nougats or creams — similar to the candies we receive in the heart shaped boxes at Valentine's Day). Frost sugar cones with green icing and decorate with peppermints, red hots, and other small candies. Invert on a bed of fresh coconut "snow" strewed with colorful foil-wrapped chocolates to create a delicious centerpiece. Place bunches of frosted grapes in bowls. Here's how to create frosted fruit: Drain washed grapes. Dip clusters into beaten egg white. Shake off excess and dip into powdered or granulated sugar. Dry on a baking rack. You can do the same with mint leaves, raspberries, strawberries, and blueberries. Serve cordials, liqueurs, champagne with strawberry floaters, and assorted coffees.

Favors

Make tutus for the brave (for those who left their tutus at home). Cut circles of tulle (a sheer nylon net usually used for bridal veils) and sew in an elastic waistband. Jazz up with glue and glitter and you're there! Everyone gets one. As the time passes — many desserts, cordials, and coffees later — everyone wears one! It's that simple.

If the sight of your boss doing a pirouette in a tutu is too much for one season, why don't you try . . .

Score Extra Points with Santa: Get a Sweet Disposition

This party is even sweeter than The Nutcracker Suite party. Yes, it's possible.

Invitations

Staple the party information to a bag of Christmas candy for each guest. Place in a gift bag filled with shredded multi-colored "candy" tissue. Or, glue the party information to a box of sugar cubes.

Attire

Your sweetest clothes.

Decorations

General Christmas. Buy some garlands of "sugar coated" plastic "candy" where Christmas decorations are sold. They look real — hang and dangle everywhere. Hang real cookie ornaments on your tree.

Menu

Your dessert spread is served on a Christmas tree. Place a large tree where the serving table would normally be. Flock with artificial snow and decorate with all sorts of sweets — cookies, candies, even twinkies; really load the tree down. Place small round tables with tablecloths that touch the floor near the tree for cakes, pies, and other desserts that can't easily hang from the tree. Spell out a Christmas greeting using sugar cubes on a cake sheet. Have a separate table set up nearby to hold napkins, plates, and utensils. This is an ideal party for a coffee bar. (*See* The Cake for details.)

Favors

Hand out boxes of Godiva chocolates, "How To Be Sweet" books, and books on "positive" attitudes. Your guests will also enjoy boxes of unique sugars, candy-coated spoons to stir in your coffee, maple and other syrups in crates and tiny jars of jams and jellies in holiday lined baskets with tiny silver spoons.

If you don't think you could be any sweeter than you already are, you're probably right!

On that positively sweet note, please remember this: You don't have to wait for a traditional holiday to celebrate. Celebrate every day! May all your days be fun days!

Resources

Where to find cool party supplies and other hot stuff.

Here's some information about companies who offer fantastic party supplies and goodies. I'd suggest contacting the companies for a copy of their latest catalog as soon as you decide you want to have a party. Seeing the merchandise that's available can prompt other ideas.

CELEBRATION FANTASTIC
1620 Montgomery Street
Suite 250
San Francisco, CA 94111
1-800-527-6566
(wine bottles with personalized labels)

COOKIE CRAFT
P.O. Box 295
Hope, NJ 07844
1-800-272-3822
(all kinds of cookie cutters)

ORIENTAL TRADING COMPANY, INC.
P.O. Box 3407
Omaha, NE 68103
1-800-228-2269, 1-402-331-6800

PERSONAL CREATIONS
530 Executive Drive
Willowbrook, IL 60514
1-800-326-6626
(Offers over 100 personalized items)

U.S. TOY CO., INC.
1227 E. 119th Street
Grandview, MO 64030
1-800-255-6124

References & Recommended Reading List

Holiday Flavors and Favors. The Junior League of Greensboro, Inc., Greensboro, North Carolina, 1975.

Holiday Food Fun. Publications International, Ltd., Lincolnwood, Illinois, 1993.

The Christmas Book of Lists: Fun-to-Read Lists & Facts about the World's Greatest Holiday, Elizabeth Haynie/ Kingsley Press, Downer Grove, Illinois, 1995.

Gober, Lasley F., *The Christmas Lovers Handbook,* Betterway Books, Cincinnati, Ohio, 1993

De Roche, Max, *The Foods of Love,* Arcade Publishing, New York, 1990

Brown, Jr.,H. Jackson, Brown, Rosemary and Peel, Kathy, *The Little Book of Christmas Joys,* Rutledge Hill Press, Nashville, Tennessee, 1995

Index

About the Author

Denise Distel Dytrych is the County Attorney for Palm Beach County, Florida. Even though this is a serious position, Denise believes that life is too short and precious to be taken seriously all the time and she strives to live every moment with this in mind. In other words, it's not all work and no play.

Her interests include health and fitness (she's a certified personal trainer), writing, traveling, and, of course, having a good time.

She lives in Tequesta, Florida with her husband, Terry, who also loves to live life to the fullest, and their two dogs, Calvin and Casey (the real party animals).

"Every day is a little life, and our whole life is but a day repeated. Therefore live every day as if it would be the last."

—Joseph Hall

"You live just once, you might as well be amusing."

—Coco Chanel

Available from Brighton Publications

Games for Party Fun by Sharon Dlugosch

Romantic At-Home Dinners: Sneaky Strategies for Couples with Kids by Nan Booth/Gary Fischler

Kid-Tastic Birthday Parties: The Complete Party Planner for Today's Kids by Jane Chase

Games for Baby Shower Fun by Sharon Dlugosch

Baby Shower Fun by Sharon Dlugosch

Reunions for Fun-Loving Families by Nancy Funke Bagley

An Anniversary to Remember: Years One to Seventy-Five by Cynthia Lueck Sowden

Folding Table Napkins: A New Look at a Traditional Craft by Sharon Dlugosch

Table Setting Guide by Sharon Dlugosch

Tabletop Vignettes by Sharon Dlugosch

Games for Wedding Shower Fun by Sharon Dlugosch, Florence Nelson

Wedding Plans: 50 Unique Themes for the Wedding of Your Dreams by Sharon Dlugosch

Wedding Hints & Reminders by Sharon Dlugosch

Wedding Occasions: 101 New Party Themes for Wedding Showers, Rehearsal Dinners, Engagement Parties, and More! by Cynthia Lueck Sowden

Dream Weddings Do Come True: How to Plan a Stress-free Wedding by Cynthia Kreuger

Don't Slurp Your Soup: A Basic Guide to Business Etiquette by Elizabeth Craig

Meeting Room Games: Getting Things Done in Committees by Nan Booth

Installation Ceremonies for Every Group: 26 Memorable Ways to Install New Officers by Pat Hines

Hit the Ground Running: Communicate Your Way to Business Success by Cynthia Kreuger

These books are available in selected stores and catalogs. If you're having trouble finding them in your area, send a self-addressed, stamped, business-size envelope and request ordering information from:

Brighton Publications, Inc.
P.O. Box 120706
St. Paul, MN 55112-0706

or call: 1-800-536-BOOK